The Path to Inner Peace

A Manual for Living in Turbulent Times

LARRY WHARTON

To order additional copies of this book, contact:
Xlibris Corporation
1-888-795-4274
www.Xlibris.com
Orders@Xlibris.com
123848

CONTENTS

Dedication

This book is dedicated to my wonderfully supportive wife,
Eleanor, and my very good friend, Pamela Matthews,
both relentlessly beneficial editors.

INTRODUCTION

Most of us at one time or another have wondered if we were truly happy, or why we were not happy much of the time. Given the challenges of today's hyper-active world, such questions are hardly surprising. What is surprising and sad is that in spite of so many people asking these important questions, the improvement in happiness has been poor at best. This book provides a path to improve the odds for people sincerely interested in finding a higher level of inner peace (used synonymously with deep happiness), and through that to live a higher quality life in all respects.

The book's title is based on two issues affecting our wellbeing. Wherever we live the external world is turbulent and likely to get more so, and many of us need a way to address this turmoil. At the same time we want to achieve a level of inner peace to aid us in dealing with our own unique inner agitation. Negotiating these challenges is extremely difficult, and having a guide to getting to inner peace can be a great help.

There are many fine books on developing inner peace, so why another one? This book is different in that it uses an eclectic approach to assist in the search for inner peace. I draw from many areas of life with the goal of integrating these areas into a unique path to inner peace for each of us. Some of this variety can be seen from the table of contents. Chapters dealing with suffering, certainty, or learning may be familiar to many readers, but the presentation and content will likely be quite new to most. Other aspects are not usually part of any book on inner peace, such as paradox, confirmatory bias, systems theory, the unconscious, the body's threat response, non-verbal communication, and two-valued reasoning, to name just a few. Drawing from diverse areas of life gives a more comprehensive perspective to both the challenges and hurdles of moving toward inner peace, and to the methods we can use to make that move.

Importantly, this book departs from some of the "normal" suggestions for gaining inner peace.

First, meditation is frequently suggested as the vehicle for gaining insight into our problems and into the process of change. Meditation aids us in slowing down our very busy minds and calming ourselves. In that sense I have personally benefitted considerably from meditation, and strongly recommend it. The difficulty is that not everyone who meditates will uncover the problematic aspects of their behavior that thwart inner peace. I know a goodly number of dedicated meditators, and few of them have arrived at the important realizations about the impediments to their inner peace, although they have benefitted in other ways.

Second, if most seekers are like me, they simply cannot by themselves achieve greater inner peace. From my experience and that of others, I have found that most of us need helpers, people who care for us and are willing to work with us through often major difficulties. And it is not just emotional support I am talking about, but the active participation of those close to us. Why we need this help and how to get it is a large part of the book's emphasis.

Third, inner peace is unlikely to be gained from reading books (this one excepted, of course!), or from attending seminars, retreats, or talks about inner peace, no matter how fine the materials or the presenter. Inner peace arises only through the development of a high level of knowledge about reality and about ourselves, and through the application of personal discipline over what is often a fairly long time, if my transition is any example. Some beneficial knowledge can sometimes be acquired through seminars, etc., but if not followed up with great discipline, it will be of little help. Later in the book I will give examples of my and others' unfortunate confusion of inputs (knowledge)with the great output of inner peace.

Beyond helping to develop inner peace that assists us in dealing well with life's ups and downs, the book emphasizes our connection with others in everyday settings where things can go quickly awry. It addresses how we can positively construct our inner lives and our outer actions so that we become a force for good with others, often influencing them in highly positive ways.

With inner peace, we can interact with people in ways that enhance both us and them. We can act constructively in a conversation gone awry. We can positively influence those with whom we are in conflict. We can assist those who are struggling with life's difficulties. But even with inner peace, we may still be unsure of how to act in a situation where we have to assist another to a more constructive interpersonal outcome. Specific challenges we all experience include dealing with a partner who does not understand that we need a bit more support with the children, uplifting a political conversation that has gone awry, addressing a friend who continually interrupts us, or dealing with someone who feels insulted by us. The techniques that aid us in moving to inner peace are the same ones that allow us to respectfully manage challenging situations with others. Part of our learning on the path to inner peace is understanding the dynamics of interpersonal difficulties, including why they arise and what can be done about them. We can then apply helpful and respectful methods that will move us and others into positive conditions.

We can all contribute to a more humane and interpersonally respectful world and leave a trail of compassion and goodness as we move through life. Compassion as I will use it refers not just to having sympathy and empathy for another's troubles, or even literally experiencing their pain. It also refers much more broadly to our deep connection with others, whether they are in pain or not. It is our ability to see them and relate to them as fellow creatures deserving of respect and care. My favorite definition of compassion is from the Dalai Lama's book, *The Art of Happiness*:

"Compassion can be roughly defined in terms of a state of mind that is nonviolent, nonharming, and nonaggressive. It is a mental attitude based on the wish for others to be free of their suffering and is associated with a sense of commitment, responsibility, and respect towards the other."

I put considerable emphasis on the connections with others in this broad sense of compassion, and I don't rely on simple nostrums to accomplish this. I use very specific behavioral aspects to illustrate what works and what does not, and why, and how all of that is intimately connected to inner peace and being a force for good. Developing this deep connection with others is difficult under the best of circumstances, but enormously more difficult when we are dealing with people whose actions or views are exceedingly challenging. Our work on inner peace asks that we understand these challenges, why they arise, and act to overcome them.

The path to inner peace asks much of us. We have to look at common-place ideas and practices in a new way, and apply them with a new vision. We have to understand the role and utility of less common-place concepts in our search for inner peace. The path is not a series of steps, but a gradual disciplined reconfiguring of our inner life and its outer expression. It is more like a framework that guides us in our search. Progress toward inner peace depends on our seeing reality for what it is, particularly seeing ourselves, with all our wonder and trouble, as we really are. The path for each of us is different because no two of us is alike, but we will all need perhaps the highest level of personal discipline of which we are capable. Seeing ourselves as we really are can be daunting, but it is the price of admission to the path. As the Spanish poet Antonio Machado said, "Wanderer, there is no path/the path is made by walking."

This book resulted from my years of work to find some level of inner peace. Writing it allowed me to clarify for myself what I had learned and how I had put that into action, including the mistakes I made in trying to get closer to inner peace. This personal work, filled with setbacks and disappointments, changed me in many ways. Importantly, I began to see a way out of the falseness of my life, out of the emotional entanglements that led me and others around me to suffer. Writing the book saved me from myself in a way, from the person I was who lived in his fantasies and entanglements, and who largely failed to see the great connection between him and others. As Mary Oliver said in her profound poem, The Journey,

> And there was a new voice
> Which you slowly
> Recognized as your own,
> That kept you company
> As you strode deeper and deeper
> Into the world,
> Determined to do
> The only thing you could do—
> Determined to save
> The only life that you could save.

The book is informed both by what I experienced in that quest and by the experiences of others: clients, friends, colleagues, and relatives. I have a strong desire to make available to others ideas and methods that are a bit off the normal but which have proven highly beneficial to me. I have made progress in my search for inner peace, but I see that search as never-ending.

The great wisdom seekers of the past and present have made it very clear that attachment is the source of all suffering. Attachment exists when we "must have" some outcome. It exists when we cannot accept the world the way it is, but instead try to alter it to fit our desires. This is a great source of suffering. The more we attempt to satisfy (feed) our attachment, the less inner peace we will have. We all have attachments, large and small, and they block our path to inner peace. Thus, moving successfully along our path requires that we deal with our attachments. Throughout the book I will talk about some of our common attachments, and among the most challenging attachments in the search for inner peace is the one we have to our stories and our views of the world.

For most of my life I lived as nearly everyone else does: "comfortable" in a world created primarily to keep me safe, a world made up of stories that were partially or wholly untrue. Just a few of the stories: I saw myself as open-minded, fair, reasonable, loving, in control of my behavior, sensible, generous, compassionate, and a good father. I was partly these things and partly not, and in the case of being in control of my behavior, not much. These illusions were all unconsciously designed to make me feel good, even though they failed to do that. But some folks have stories that make them feel bad, such as I am too fat or not smart enough; mother never really loved me; I cannot make friends; I am a loser. Positive or negative, the problem is that the stories are often mostly or totally false, and it is our clinging to them that creates suffering for us and others.

Part of my story telling included concepts about the way the world worked (really the way I wanted the world to work). These were seriously or totally at odds with reality. Some of my examples: that the world is made up of discrete elements which have no connection with each other, that there is a right way and a wrong way to do everything, that people who disagreed with me were not very bright, that my answers were always correct, that religious people were crazy, that life should be fair, and that pain does not have to be part of life.

My stories caused me and others suffering, and the whole while I was completely unaware of this. I lived my stories, my illusions, as though they were completely real. I saw my world as real and everyone else's (at least those folks who disagreed with me) as unreal and wrong. My attachments harmed people because I saw everything in either/or terms—my way or the highway. Even if I was polite in disagreeing with others, which I generally wasn't, they still felt the certainty of my convictions and the dismissal of their ideas.

Moving beyond our false beliefs to inner peace is nearly impossible unless we live as much as we can in the present moment. Being in the present moment we are attentive, not to the future nor to the past, but to this instant now. Whatever we are doing we want to be doing only that one thing. We could be sweeping the floor or meditating or giving a speech, and we are not distracted by other thoughts, emotions, or actions. We are simultaneously monitoring our inner and outer worlds with the goal of being totally present. Being in the present moment is also referred to as being mindful, in which we are attending only to the "now" without judgment, without liking or disliking what is happening and without reacting, a key aspect of inner peace.

When we distract ourselves from the present moment by failing to attend to what is happening around us, we are "elsewhere," and unaware of possibly doing harm to others. A person talking on the phone while driving is distracted, even if only slightly, and that can easily disrupt the traffic movement of other drivers. Or a person who walks up to two people already in conversation and interrupts them, turning his attention to one of the two conversants and ignoring the other. Neither the driver nor the interrupter is thinking about the well being of others, only about what he/she must do (a "must have" outcome). They are both out of the present moment and distracted, and thus harm to others is a real possibility.

Being distracted for any reason presents a big problem for our growth: it keeps us from uncovering who we are, from understanding the false stories we tell, our attachments, and the adverse impact on others. Any distractions allow us to avoid the hard look at our own illusions and our own suffering, thus keeping us from inner peace. Being in the present moment is so important in our search for inner peace and being a force for good that it is part of every chapter in the book.

Many who desire greater inner peace will not be able to achieve it. What brings one person to the realization that his/her present existence cannot continue, and who then still does nothing about it? What brings another person to the same realization, and who then embarks on and stays with the very difficult process of gaining inner peace? There is no clear answer to this. Perhaps when we have suffered enough, the movement occurs. Or, perhaps when our mind, in one special moment clear as a bell and unencumbered by our everyday cognitive and emotional mess, sees what it has been unable to see before. Something or a group of things is a trigger, but we are unlikely to ever know what it is for any one person, and it does not matter.

This book will not protect readers' sensitivities. In fact, if those sensitivities are not disturbed and bruised at least a little, little progress can be made. Learning means to acquire knowledge and then to apply it, holding on through the disequilibrium and upsets that entails. If there is no discomfort in that process, there will be no learning, which means there will be no personal change. This is particularly true in moving toward inner peace because we have so many years of existence in our "comfortable" world. Upsetting that world is very threatening for most people; it certainly was for me. But no upset, no progress.

Each chapter addresses a part of the whole that represents each of our paths. The early chapters in particular address the many hurdles we may face in moving toward inner peace. Even reading about these significant hurdles, not to mention engaging them, can be discouraging and daunting. But there is no way to avoid or go around this experience. We can only go through it. Thus, the book and the challenges it presents mimic life in which trying to avoid reality (the difficulties of moving toward inner peace) creates suffering.

The first four chapters show why our thoughts, emotions and actions have not helped us gain inner peace. Chapter 1 examines what inner peace is and is not, and then emphasizes that we can make a choice to have inner peace or suffering. Chapter 2 looks at the big challenge presented by the need to be certain, and how the fear of vulnerability and self-consciousness impede our move to inner peace. Chapter 3 emphasizes that we cannot easily move to inner peace without understanding that learning entails being out of balance, in a state of disequilibrium that is often very uncomfortable. Chapter 4 addresses transience and change and how trying to defeat those, trying to make the world different than it is, leads only to suffering.

The next four chapters address critical practical aspects of how to move to inner peace. Chapter 5 presents the vital connection between those who care for us and their specific aid in our movement down the path of inner peace. It gives clear and specific advice as to how to approach and interact with our helpers. Chapter 6 challenges us to see the power of paradox and how that understanding can aid in our effort to walk the path of inner peace and connect well with others. Chapter 7 addresses how to have uplifting and respectful conversations no matter how difficult the circumstances. Sample dialogues illustrate how to "manage" difficult conversations. The conclusion is Chapter 8, which brings us to the vital appreciation that making progress on the path to inner peace allows us to develop compassion and wisdom, the two great pillars of the uplifted life.

To help in the understanding of particular points I am making, I will use examples from my life and from the lives of others. Occasionally I will use quotes to challenge your thinking. I will also use short dialogues to illustrate how people demonstrate the presence or absence of inner peace in their relations with others. I place particular emphasis on how to create connections with others that are uplifting for everyone, and throughout the book I will make suggestions on how to move forward successfully toward that goal.

How will the reader benefit from this book? That is up to each person. But I hope that any reader will gain an appreciation for the subtleties that underlie our problematic behavior and cause suffering for us and others. I hope the reader will see how entrenched and powerful our illusions are, and that we can alter those. I further hope that the path elements coupled with personal discipline will lead to changes in how readers view themselves and the world such that they acquire a greater degree of inner peace. And I hope that readers will be able to apply this new inner peace to their relationships, improving those dramatically. While this book is about gaining inner peace, it is at least as much about living a better and more compassionate life, and about positively influencing others by modeling that life, about living a life of wisdom.

CHAPTER 1

Inner Peace or Suffering, It's Our Choice

What exactly is inner peace? For much of my life I thought I knew, but a lot of what I imagined was wrong. The part I got right was appreciating that inner peace is an internal state. The part I got wrong was thinking that I could acquire that internal state by finding places where I could "relax." My view was simple: If I could only sit at the ocean and read books on Eastern wisdom I would be happy and have inner peace. Naturally, on those occasions when I got to the ocean I was indeed relaxed, at least for a while, but I did not acquire any inner peace. I had associated reading and relaxing with inner peace. No wonder that I failed to acquire it.

What characteristics do people with inner peace have? How can we know them and, for our own development, what can we look for in ourselves?

People with inner peace possess a state of deep equanimity, expressed by a balanced, non-judgmental response to the world. These individuals have no need for the world to be different than it is. They accept the world fully without the need to hold onto the things they like or push away the things they don't like. They do not impose arbitrary characteristics on the world, as in this thing or experience is good and that is bad. They respond comfortably to life's ups and downs, often with humor even when they are in the midst of a major trial. Such people have light hearts, and live harmoniously with reality. There is a calmness and solidity about those with inner peace, and the sense that they cannot be shoved off balance very easily. Importantly for proper action, those with inner peace see the world as connection, not separateness, allowing them to experience a broad sense of compassion and thus be a force for good.

Those with inner peace have the ability to become aware of, monitor, and manage their inner states. We are all subject to unpleasant experiences and the resulting negative thoughts and emotions. The idea of managing is not one of forcing our thoughts or emotions to do as we want, nor of stifling them in any way. It is about recognizing, acknowledging, and accepting them, and then gently moving our attention elsewhere when we have negative emotions or thoughts. While difficult to do in the beginning, the more we practice managing the easier it gets, until those negative aspects have very little energy and intrude hardly at all into our lives. Having inner peace means we change the content of our consciousness so that we see, interpret, and act on the world in the most beneficial manner no matter how difficult a situation may be.

Managing our internal state and the actions flowing from them depend on our being in the present moment. As we monitor our internal state, we also simultaneously attend to our connection with those around us. Only if we exist in the present moment can we effectively monitor our emotions, thoughts, and actions, thereby ensuring our actions are appropriate and that we are a force for good.

Acting appropriately, with care and respect for others, expresses the quality of our internal state of inner peace. What we are inside shows itself outside in how we deal with everyday life and how we act towards others. As our inner peace increases we are more at ease with the world, even with people with whom we might have differences. More inner peace means a soft and easy connection with others, a high sensitivity to others' well-being characterized by humility. The greater our inner peace the more able we are to assist others, especially in challenging settings. As we express care for others they are more likely to trust us, which then enables us to more easily be a force for good.

I like to think of inner peace as inner clarity, which is the purity of our connection to reality unencumbered by distortions such as our false stories, likes and dislikes, and attachments. The purer our connection to reality, the greater our inner peace. We have inner clarity when our emotions, thoughts, and actions align with what is. Just as we can bring a camera lens into finer focus, we can also bring our own inner "seeing" into finer focus, free from the obscurity and ambiguity of our attachments. Those with inner peace "know" intuitively what the proper response to any situation is, and this is clarity. Further, exporting our inner peace by assisting others in finding greater clarity, without attempting to change or control them, is part of how we show compassion and respect for others.

To help narrow the focus of what inner peace is, some of this chapter is devoted to what it is not, to clarifying the confusions we may have about its nature. The chapter also addresses the suffering arising from the false stories we tell and the negative role of attachment in our search for inner peace.

Perhaps the most common misunderstanding is to see inner peace as pleasure. Pleasure is a fine thing in many cases, but it is short-lived. We can experience pleasure from sex, food, alcohol, the athletic high of winning, watching a great singer perform, reading a fine book, playing with our child, watching a funny movie, getting a compliment from our boss, and so forth. Such small joys and pleasures are the stuff of our daily lives and it is natural to enjoy them. However, we must be aware that even these joys can be the stuff of trouble if we are attached to them, if we "must have" them. Inner peace is a fundamental attitude toward the world that is not upset by things going poorly nor absorbed by desire that wonderful pleasures stay around forever.

Inner peace is not about money, power, prestige, or accomplishment. As with pleasure, there is nothing inherently problematic with these. Even power, if used well and in the service of others, is fine. The difficulty arises when people equate these with inner peace. Since our world is filled with ups and downs, our money, power, prestige or accomplishments can change in a moment's notice. Thus, they cannot provide us with inner peace, which is not subject to life's positive and negative movements. We have all known people who imagine, even if only in their unconscious, that inner peace will arrive if only they get that next raise, or more control over their spouse, or a particular award, etc.

Inner peace is not freedom from troubles. It is not freedom from pain, losses, disappointments, sickness, or mistakes. It is not about living in some ideal condition in which there are no challenges or unpleasant real world interventions in our lives. Inner peace is not a diversion or separation from life's ups and downs. This understanding is critical because the search for inner peace is filled with nice happenings and not-so-nice happenings. A person with inner peace is neither attached to the nice aspects (I wish this beautiful sunset would never end) nor attached to the desire to get rid of the not-so-nice aspects (I wish my terrible neighbor would move).

And inner peace is not developed by acquiring or having "things." There is nothing at all wrong with having a nice home, beautiful cars, a good job, wonderful children, a stimulating political association, or a comforting religious affiliation. As rewarding and enjoyable as these can be, they are not the stuff of inner peace, which cannot be acquired outside ourselves. Enjoying and taking advantage of "externals" is perfectly fine so long as we do not expect them to produce inner peace.

Seeing inner peace as something that it is not compromises our search. My sense that I could acquire inner peace if only I was able to read Eastern wisdom at the ocean is a good example of misunderstanding both what inner peace is and how it is acquired. Our search is also compromised because we live much of our lives as illusions made up of our false stories. And we are often quite attached to these stories. When we bump up against life, things and people that challenge us, we explain those interactions and our responses in ways that protect our very powerful stories. We continually reinforce the stories and this blocks our path to inner peace. We have no idea what is happening or why, but we "know" that we are not the problem. The problem is "out there."

We often judge our current condition based on what we are thinking, what our conscious mind is telling us—the stories. If I think I am happy, a good parent, a reasonable boss, self-aware, open to new things, a quality friend, etc., then I am, even if none of these is true. What we think, we believe, often to our detriment. If the world sends us messages that such views are at least partially false (which it is doing continuously), it makes no difference. These important messages about our stories cannot get through. We literally cannot hear or accept them, and our move to inner peace is compromised. When those valuable messages fail to make it through, we suffer.

There was a wonderful book written in the late 1880's called, *Flatland*, by Edwin A. Abbott.

The story is about a completely flat world where all the inhabitants are geometric shapes of two dimensions. In other words, the inhabitants have no concept of a third dimension. A sphere arrives and the flatlanders can see only its two-dimensional image of a circle. The sphere tries to convince a particular flatlander that the world is more than he sees, to no avail. Seeing no other option, the sphere pulls the flatlander out of his world into the third dimension, the latter shrieking with fear, "Either this is madness or it is hell." The sphere responds, "It is neither; it is knowledge; it is three dimensions: open your eye once again and try to look steadily."

Can we look steadily?

Some years ago my wife, Eleanor, and I were in couples' counseling. In one session I made what I thought was an important point to her. She responded as though she did not hear what I said. I asked the therapist for help. He repeated what I had said and asked Eleanor if she had heard me. She said no. Later Eleanor told me that her inability to hear was the result of what she had learned to do as a child to protect herself: she learned to hide inside herself, the only place of safety. While the hiding response was needed as a child, it now represented a false story. My wife did not disregard what I had said. She did not hear it and then dismiss it. She literally did not hear it. It never registered. That information could not get in because of her fear. This insight was very difficult for my wife to absorb, but it represented her willingness to "look steadily" at something that was very fearful.

Paradoxically, those of us seeking inner peace must look at things we cannot see, and often cannot even conceive of! My own revelation in counseling shook me considerably. In the midst of talking about the difficulties my wife and I were having in resolving conflict, an extremely unpleasant thought blasted me: I did not trust women's emotions. This shocked me because my story was that I both respected and trusted women. That story was false in a big way. My mistrust had to do with my own upbringing and the manipulation used by my mother and aunts with each other and with me. I never knew I distrusted women and that led to some of the difficulties my wife and I were having.

The insights my wife and I had were critically important to our moving forward as a couple into a more respectful relationship, and for each of us to move forward in the search for inner peace. We had to "look steadily" at very unpleasant things, and not blink. A large challenge for both of us was to see that all our lives we had lived as though a certain story were true, when it was not. We each played out a false story to which we were totally attached, and were completely unaware of the unpleasantness we were causing. I came at the relationship from a place of distrust and she of fear. Not understanding that, we both acted in ways that caused the other suffering.

We all suffer, but that does not have to be our lot. To move successfully to inner peace we have to understand what suffering is and how it is self-generated. The path to inner peace is how we reduce and eventually eliminate suffering, both for ourselves and for others.

As I mentioned in the Introduction, suffering arises out of attachment, out of being in a "must have" state. I am not talking about a normal wanting of something. When we are attached, the "must have" is unbelievably powerful and often awakens very strong emotions, ones of which we are only dimly aware or even totally unaware. Attachments reflect emotional disturbance resulting from the fear that things are not going as we want. We can be attached to positions, views, desires, ideas, actions, relationships, material goods, anything that will give us even a small sense of stability or avoidance of difficulty. Sadly, this clinging provides only the illusion of stability and of control, and it creates suffering for us and others because we act on those attachments.

One of the attachments I am working on arises when I am at the grocery store. If I see someone else moving his/her cart toward a checkout counter, any checkout counter, I have a fear sensation in the middle of my chest. That person will get to the checkout counter before me! I am attached to being first in line (interesting psychology here!), and this causes me suffering. The same emotional/physical experience happens whenever I sense I am not going to get my share of something. I am emotionally upset, although for decades I denied it, arguing that I was simply desiring to move along efficiently. I am emotionally hooked by my attachment, and am working to change that.

Imagine that we want a promotion at work. Doing everything legitimate and moral to get it is not a problem. However, a problem could be our attachment to the outcome, which may dictate inappropriate or even illegal behavior. Not getting the promotion means disappointment, as does even the sense that we might not get it, and this is normal. We become attached when we use underhanded and manipulative techniques in an effort to get the promotion, or when we allow the loss (or possible loss) of the promotion to develop into a victim (or sour grapes) mentality, one characterized by self-pity.

In the first situation, the attachment to the promotion is so powerful that any tactic or method is acceptable. In responding to an attachment, we will often justify our actions after the fact to make our behavior palatable to ourselves. We will suffer from the emotional turmoil (fear, anxiety, frustration, anger, etc.) that arises when we sense we might not get the promotion or the disappointment that comes from not getting it. The fact that we often do not experience these emotions at the conscious level does not at all mean they are not there. And they will exact a toll.

When we don't get the promotion there may be a victim attitude: "Poor, poor me, I didn't get the promotion. I deserved it. I am better than that moron they chose for it. Fate kicked me again. Why can't I ever win?" It is abundantly clear that we are creating our own suffering. We are attached to getting the promotion, and we are just as attached to the idea of being a victim, to self pity. When we think and act this way, we often see every issue that confronts us as further confirmation of victimhood. Every conversation we have about the challenges we experience is presented, both in words and tone of voice, precisely the same: poor me. This attachment to the victim state creates large amounts of suffering.

Above I mentioned after-the-fact rationalizations of our behavior. For much of my life I was an angry person, although I denied it. I had disagreements with people, even those close to me, and my anger would surface and people would notice. Once I was having a political argument with a friend and I got angry. With some concern he asked me why I was angry. I responded that I was not angry at all, just enthusiastic, to which he replied that it sure looked like anger to him. At that moment I believed what I was saying, that I was showing only enthusiasm. Later, much later, I realized I was indeed angry, mainly because I did not like his disagreeing with me. I was attached to getting my way, and I suffered because I was not getting it. With my anger I was unconsciously trying to export my suffering to him, but fortunately for him he was having none of it. Regrettably, it took decades for me to realize that I was living a false story.

Consider a simple but very common bump against reality. I was sitting in a coffee shop not long ago and a man was on his cell phone talking about some complex business arrangement. He was speaking quite loudly, even getting up out of his chair and wandering around the shop during the conversation. He was clearly focusing all his attention on this call, for which he was eminently in the present moment. The problem: he was not in the present moment for the rest of us in the coffee shop, thus failing to take the well-being of others into account and being unable to act as a force for good.

Another bump: Once while I was driving a school bus pulled out in front of me from a side street. There was no real danger, but I had to either brake or move out of the lane I was in. As I drove past the bus I could see that the driver had no idea of what just happened, just as the man in the coffee shop likely did not. Both were momentarily absent from the present moment and took action without considering the impact on others. The "harm" of those actions was very small, but it is just such acts, thoughtlessly executed while we are distracted, that creates troubles for others.

The coffee shop and bus examples illustrate a very important aspect of attachment, not all which is accompanied by mental and emotional anguish. The man in the coffee shop and the bus driver did not likely experience any suffering as result of their actions. But both of them were distracted from the present moment and attached to that distraction, attached to their current mental or emotional state. Being "elsewhere" and unconnected to others near them, they exported difficulties.

People in the coffee shop certainly had choices, mainly to do something about the loud talking or not. If not, then acceptance without recriminations is fine. This was the avenue I took, mainly because it required me to deal with any desire to make things different. It required me to practice my inner peace, which I very much needed in this situation as I "want" the coffee shop to be a quiet place. Taking action, such as talking with the man or mentioning the situation to the manager, is not a problem so long as we are not attached to getting our way and relate to the other in a caring and respectful manner.

Imagine I want something as simple as to have the TV controller and change the "stupid" channel my spouse is watching. Oh, come on, what's the big deal, things like this happen to everyone. They do indeed happen to everyone and the issue does not have to be a big deal to be a big deal. It can be a tiny deal, but attachment makes it a very big event, one that essentially destroys relationships over time as one "small deal" follows another. What matters is how badly I "must have" the outcome, and what I will do to get it. In the grip of my attachment to getting my way, I act-out, perhaps by making a demeaning remark about what my spouse is watching. Perhaps by telling her with powerful emotional emphasis that I need to watch a special program and she has to give up what she is watching for me. Or, perhaps even by removing the TV controller from her hand. None of these actions will turn out well for either party. My actions say clearly to my wife that I will get my way; controlling her is now the issue. Such "simple" interactions are the stuff of which suffering is made. I suffer because of my need to have control and my spouse may suffer as well because I misbehave: suffering exported.

My wife has used a chiropractor for years. I have considered them to be near charlatans (less so now), and not worth anything. She insisted that certain physical back and neck issues of hers were helped by the chiropractor. I was irritated with her view, and felt that using the chiropractor was simply a way to get an expensive massage that was of no real physical benefit. I attempted to maintain equanimity while talking with her about the chiropractor, but I failed. Even though I used what I thought were rational arguments, my frustration came out non-verbally time and time again, clearly upsetting her, and producing no good at all. I was attached to the need to get her to stop using the chiropractor, for her to see the light (see things my way). Because of that I suffered and so did she. I had to work hard for some time to overcome my need to get her to do what I wanted.

In the last two examples, I emphasized control, especially control of others. The story about the TV remote clearly indicates a control issue, as does mine regarding the chiropractor. Many people I know have big issues around control; that is, they want to control their world and other people, to make the universe conform to their desires and "must haves." However, most people dislike the idea of being controlled and resist, creating yet more suffering for everyone. When we are in controller mode, we are attached to getting our way through any methods available. This means a bad outcome for the person we are seeking to control. We cannot see that our behavior and our methods (usually manipulation of some kind, if not outright force) are damaging to the other person as well as to us. We only "see" that we "must have" what we want. Yet more suffering.

It is not only particular outcomes or interpersonal engagements that bring out attachment. Ideas or views or values can also be problematic. You need only to listen to most people's comments about politics to see attachment. They describe their own views and positions, and those of their party, candidate, or favorite group, as essentially correct in all ways. The "others," people of different political views or positions, are not only wrong on all counts, but also likely to be characterized (demonized) as immoral creatures as well. The demonizers are absolutely convinced of the correctness of all of their views. Absolute certainty is a sure sign of a major attachment, and I address this in the next chapter. When in the grip of certainty we have a very low capacity for reflective and objective thought, even though we are fully convinced we are quite objective. Yet another false story. We are simply, but profoundly, unable to give fair weight to the views of others. Naturally, this creates a lot of suffering.

Many people think suffering is about pain, and it can be. But I am not talking about pain directly. It's what we do with any pain, whether it is physical, emotional or spiritual, that exists in our lives every day. As we bump up against obstacles to our inner peace, we experience discomfort (pain) and we make an effort to create the outcomes we want, to remove the pain and get the desired state back. "I will get that promotion" creates an emotional condition that governs everything. "I need that channel changed" does precisely the same thing. It is the "must have" condition that creates the suffering. It is not the understandable desire to have a promotion or to change the channel, which we might see as pain. Nor is it the equally understandable feeling of disappointment of not getting the promotion. It is the sense that we must have our way or very bad things will happen that creates the suffering. Pain is a fact of life. Suffering does not have to be.

When we have acquired inner peace we are not affected by what happens to us, whether it is good or bad. We have formulated our world such that we do not make evaluations of, nor are we attached to, what is good and what is bad. It isn't that we have no negative feelings, like being disappointed, fearful, anxious, or angry. All of us experience such emotions, including people with inner peace. The huge difference is what we do with those emotions. Instead of allowing the emotions to dictate behavior, we accept and acknowledge the feelings. If we cling to those feelings, or try to force them away, we will give them energy, and this will obstruct moving to inner peace. After accepting and acknowledging the feelings, we then allow those emotions to float away by moving our attention to more positive places, with no force or energy required. This gentle redirecting of emotions (and unpleasant thoughts) is a vital form of discipline, of managing our emotions and thoughts.

Such mental and emotional discipline is not the same as positive self-talk, which has been shown to be of very limited value. Simply substituting a good thought for a not-so-good thought is insufficient and of little use because we are attempting to control our thoughts, which actually gives the negative elements even more energy. The critical aspect is accepting and acknowledging our less-than-desirable thoughts, and not reacting to them. Only then we can move our attention to more positive and uplifting thoughts and emotions.

Dan Millman, in his fine book, *Wisdom of the Peaceful Warrior*, says our emotions may be "telling" us to do one thing that is not particularly beneficial, but our mental discipline can over-ride that. We may be feeling irritated at the very moment when compassion is needed. Dan tells us to act compassionately regardless of what our emotions tell us. We are in "control" of our lives when we can do this without effort or force. We develop greater inner peace as a result because we are able to monitor our thinking and emotions, and then take proper action (in this case acting compassionately). It is this level of mental and emotional discipline that can produce the inner peace we all desire as well as beneficial outcomes for others.

Having inner peace means that we also experience pleasurable states and emotions such as joy, exhilaration, and delight, but we do not cling to those states just as we do not cling to getting rid of unpleasant ones. We do not expect or even want those experiences to continue forever. We understand the way the world really works, that nothing lasts. Needing good times to last creates suffering. What really matters is the present moment of experience and our connection to that. Being in the present moment creates the conditions by which we can allow any negative thoughts or emotions to evaporate, to leave without causing us or others any suffering.

To quote from Dan Millman (he uses a "fictional" character named Socrates to advise a young athlete): "If you don't get what you want, you suffer; if you get what you don't want, you suffer; even when you get exactly what you want, you still suffer because you can't hold on to it forever." This encapsulates beautifully the essence of attachment and suffering.

Suffering is not pain, which is a natural part of life and results from the setbacks, injuries, disappointments, illnesses, and so forth we all experience. Pain does not create suffering, which is a choice we make, even when we are not conscious of making it. Suffering does not exist until we bring it into existence. Suffering is the result of allowing ourselves to be affected, often hugely, by what happens to us, trying to hold onto the nice things and to get rid of those we don't like. When we have inner peace we still experience the pain of disappointment, sadness, fear, loss, and anxiety. The difference is that we do not stay with these emotions; we do not hold on to or wallow in them. That is what creates suffering.

It is we who have created our stories and attachments and we can get rid of them—if we want to. We all have the option, at every moment, of changing the content of our consciousness, of seeing the world as it truly is, not as we want it to be. We can choose suffering or we can choose inner peace. The choice is entirely ours.

CHAPTER 2

The Tyranny of Certainty

Among the many challenges we face today is the fact that our world is moving faster and faster. There are other challenges, but this one in particular dramatically heightens our disorientation and emotional difficulty. We have the sense that there is nothing sure, nothing solid to hold onto. Control has been lost. As things move faster we are continuously distracted, jumping with ever more speed from one thing to another. We are unable to sustain attentiveness and balance, to maintain existence in the present moment. The acceleration of change engenders fear as more of life seems unknown, even unknowable, and there is a profound sense of unpredictability in the world.

We are also challenged by the apparent loss of many of the norms that used to bind us together. Emile Durkheim, the great sociologist, coined a word for this condition, anomie, meaning normlessness. With anomie the rules governing how we should treat each other have broken down, and we are unsure of what to expect from others. This produces fear and anxiety, made worse by the fact that we have no clear understanding of what is going on or of how to deal with these difficult societal conditions. From a Gallup poll in 1994 (things may be worse since then), Americans said that, ". . . these days a person doesn't really know whom he can count on."

Exist in this disorienting and fearful state for very long and we begin to look for anything that will get us back in control. We will grasp at whatever looks like a life preserver, putting some stability back in our life. Regrettably, the anxiety of being without a firm sense of inner foundation often pushes us to find problematic sources of stability, such as excessive use of sex, drugs, TV, food, shopping, cell-phone or internet usage, texting, work or even efforts at enlightenment. And among the more destructive excesses is trying to find refuge from the sea of chaos in certainty. Certainty gives the illusion that we are back in control of our lives, but it actually obstructs the path to inner peace.

Not all certainty is a problem. For instance, I am certain that my wife loves me. I am certain that the sun will rise in the east tomorrow. I am certain that my friends will be there for me in times of trial. Is it possible these are false beliefs? Yes, possibly. Their truth is demonstrated often and this tends to confirm the validity of my belief, even if it is not proven conclusively. Having a sense of certainty, as these three examples illustrate, is not the same as having the need to be certain. A normal sense of certainty is necessary to get through life. If everything, including whether our cars will start tomorrow, is subject to significant unpredictability and lack of certainty, we would be paralyzed.

The most damaging and pervasive way we exhibit we are in the grip of the need to be certain is that anyone who disagrees with us is dead wrong. When we are in this state, our world is like a box with impermeable sides and us at the center. Only things that confirm our views get through, a psychological dynamic known as confirmatory bias. Information that is not in agreement cannot be allowed in, and the exclusion is unconscious. Those who bring such information have to be dealt with, often very harshly.

When we need to be certain we are generally not aware of behaving in problematic ways. Encountering people with whom we disagree, we see only reactions from them that are challenging, often mystifying, and always wrong. Stress arises and we must act. This action is often taken using one or more of three general tactics, all of which have one goal: to make us right and the other wrong, to reinforce the certainty and correctness of our view. These tactics are widespread and I have seen these often in myself and many others.

In the grip of certainty, one or more of the three general unpleasant tactics is used: Attack, Defend, and Deflect, often accompanied by considerable emotion. The motive for all three tactics is identical. Order and control have to be restored because some part of our story about how the world works has been disturbed by new information, usually presented by another person who is in our "way." What we are certain about is mainly irrelevant. It could as easily be about religion as about sports; about opera as about sewage systems.

Attacking occurs when we vigorously criticize others, actively rejecting their views, and often rejecting them as persons. One goal in this effort may be to make sure they know that they are wrong without a very good reason, to inform them of the error of their thinking. Another goal may be to change the others' views. And a third goal could be to punish them. This last is very common but often heatedly denied by those doing it. I am very familiar with this goal as I have used it extensively. Attacking often has considerable emotion attached to it, making for an even messier situation that produces only suffering all around. And, of course, attacking is also a means of avoiding a fair and open conversation about our differences.

As attackers we use whatever methods allow us to win, to restore the "order" that was lost with the introduction of new information. Such methods include anger, sarcasm, guilt, yelling, accusations, misrepresentation, condescension, "facts," outright lies, ridicule, interruption, name-calling, victimization, categorical denials or assertions, etc. These actions appear to get us back in control. The more intense our need for certainty, the more dramatic we will act out to win and the more suffering there will be. And all of these methods are very useful when we want to punish anyone who disagrees with us. Of course there can be polite engagements. But even with politeness, whatever methods are used often have that one big end: to make us right and the other wrong. The other person always senses that an unfair interaction is going on and responds accordingly, making matters worse.

I recall numerous examples from the past when my wife or I used attacks on each other. Once she told me in an argument that I did not listen. I immediately said she was wrong and that she didn't listen either. On another occasion I told her that she used negative non-verbal signals, such as a sarcastic tone of voice. She denied doing so and accused me of using a similar method, a "lecturing" tone. The fact that each of us did in fact use those techniques mattered not at all. Take a hit and give one right back.

We are defending when we "explain" why another is incorrect, and it is often used when we want to avoid dealing with a difficult issue. A very common example of this tactic among partners or spouses or friends occurs when we tell the other person we are upset about something.

Wife: I am upset that you agreed to take out the garbage every day and have hardly done that.
Husband: Why do you not understand the work pressure on me?
Wife: What does that have to do with your taking out the garbage?
Husband: It should be obvious that I do not have the time or the energy to take it out all the time.

The real message the wife gets is that his agreement to take out the garbage became null and void when it was inconvenient. Even if his arguments are legitimate and he is pressured at work, a proper conversation would address his commitment to her and her concern. Instead he accuses her of lacking any understanding of his problems. He gives no appreciation to the fact that she is correct in her concern about the garbage and has every right to bring it up. The husband has cleverly and harmfully turned the situation around to where he is now the victim of her not appreciating his work pressures. The wife ends of up with an accusation of insensitivity and no resolution to the garbage issue. Suffering.

Deflecting (also diverting) is like defending, but it is more an attempt to move the conversation to a place, any place, where we can prevail. In the example above of the garbage, deflecting might involve the husband saying that the wife failed to call his mother on her birthday. This tactic allowed him to do two things: move the issue to one that is irrelevant to the wife's actual concern (the garbage), and attack her for something he is upset about. But what if in this case the husband is correct, and the wife did fail to call his mother on her birthday? What meaning does that have? Zero at the moment. The husband has received information from his wife about an issue that is bothering her. That issue should have been dealt with openly and fairly before his issue was. Deflecting allowed the husband to avoid a difficulty he should have addressed with his wife at the time. It also allowed him to raise something that has been bothering him. Nothing wrong with the latter, but the wife's issue has to be respectfully dealt with first.

Using one or more of the three tactics allows us to win and the other to lose. These tactics have nothing to do with one person being factually correct. The problem is the need to be correct or right, to be certain. Most "conversations" and arguments in everyday life are conducted with the agenda of getting control and winning. Each of us uses one or more of the tactics and strenuously resists the often corresponding efforts of the other party. Frustration and anger increase as neither of us gets what we want. Even if by chance the "conversation" is conducted with some level of politeness, it still goes nowhere. There is no understanding of difference, much less effective resolution of it, only a large waste of human energy and increased suffering. There is no "winning" when we use unpleasant and disrespectful tactics. Even if we prevail, we do not win. We have merely managed to export our troubles to others.

I have a friend who must critique anything with which he disagrees, immediately. He responds very calmly and politely, and thus it seems hard to assess this as an attack. He responds to the first statement the person makes as though that were the entire essence of what the person is saying. He appears certain that he understands the issue completely and thus has little interest in inquiry (questions) which will help him see the full nature of what the person is saying. I am not suggesting that his critique is necessarily factually wrong. But his approach means the "conversation" could easily turn into an adversarial one, rather than into one that will elevate both parties' understanding of what is usually a complex issue. His style of critique is friendly, but it is still based on him maintaining control of the "conversation," which allows him to win.

As we move to inner peace, the need for certainty will recede and we will behave less and less frequently in ways that try to control others or get outcomes we "must have." Further, such progress allows us to deal respectfully with others' needs for certainty and control, and that is the subject of Chapter 7.

Defensiveness can occur at any time and with any of the three tactics, and it is different from defending. Defensiveness is an emotional reaction which is the unconscious's way of reducing anxiety and protecting the conscious from unpleasant thoughts or feelings. It keeps us in control of the situation. Defensive reactions are instantaneous, automatic, and unconscious at the moment of action. They are almost always accompanied by visible negative emotion. The specific goal of defensive reactions is to protect us from criticism, exposure of our shortcomings, or other real or perceived threats. Defensive reactions are attachments as their goal is to keep us "safe" from reality, to ensure that we will not have to deal with any unpleasantness. The reaction does not arise from the conscious mind, although our conscious mind might well justify our defensive reaction and inappropriate behavior with after-the-fact arguments.

It is important to know what defensiveness looks and sounds like, in ourselves and others. Non-verbal actions are the main way defensiveness is shown. They include tone of voice (accusatory, angry, sarcastic, dismissive), yelling, finger-waving and pointing, interrupting, aggressive body posturing, sighs, eye-rolls, etc. It can also be shown by silence, or withdrawal from the discussion. These actions, coupled with those mentioned earlier above, are what nearly all of us do to some extent when we feel threatened, when we are in the grip of an attachment. Knowing we may have these unpleasant reactions is vital because we could demonstrate them in the work with our helper (covered in Chapter 5), the person who cares for us and who will assist us in moving on the path to inner peace. Such demonstrations could cause problems for our helper, the last thing we want as we move to inner peace.

Certainty provides a sense of solidity, but it is an illusion and can cause us to act in ways harmful to ourselves and to others. Our certainty needs are driven by the necessity to have things back in control, although we cannot perceive that. What we know is that things are not going our way. I mentioned two major societal challenges at the start of this chapter, the increased pace of life and societal anomie. These challenges (and others unique to each person) have pushed many of us to behavior that gives a sense, even if illusory, of control of our lives, and is thus very seductive. Sadly, this attachment fails to give us a long-term sense of well-being and makes our relations with others worse as we attempt yet again to force the world to do what we want.

Needing to be certain, to be in control, means we avoid vulnerability. At one level, this is reasonable, as none of us wants to be susceptible to attack or censure. Vulnerability in another more subtle sense is part of the path to inner peace. An interesting paradox: we can be both vulnerable and not vulnerable at the same time and still be firmly on the path to inner peace. The subtle sense of vulnerability asks that we open ourselves to the falseness of our stories and the damage of our attachments. It asks that we intentionally expose ourselves to challenging and often unpleasant information about ourselves. It asks that we recognize that we know little and can be certain of less. It asks that we take an unsupported leap into uncertainty and discomfort.

For decades I protected myself with an image of invulnerability using false stories, attempting to convince myself and others that I was something other than I was. Sadly, my false stories were very effective; they kept me from having to deal with issues that I feared. Of course, I had no direct knowledge of this fear, and was thus "blissfully" unenlightened. One aspect in particular was very troubling for me and others, my anger.

I could see that my anger caused others problems, but I justified it by telling myself the story that men get angry, and that was natural. More importantly, if I got angry it was because someone had screwed up. Only after many years of therapy did I come to understand that I was intimidating people so that they caved in to my anger. It got me what I wanted. I never saw this, and my anger became part of how I "managed" my relations with others. Getting what I wanted was very important. But at least as important was that my anger helped me avoid dealing with important challenging issues and circumstances. Anger kept people and unpleasant issues at bay. No vulnerability for me!

My anger shielded me from having to open myself to some very unpleasant things. We all have our own unique ways of keeping vulnerability at bay, of staying certain in our false stories. Some evidence of our active avoidance of vulnerability:

- We find it difficult to apologize.
- We push ourselves to the front, lacking humility.
- We are overly sensitive to anything, especially insults, real or imagined.
- We have difficulty revealing negative things about ourselves.
- We have no or little sense of humor about ourselves, taking ourselves very seriously.
- We need to have an answer for everything and that answer must be correct.
- We are unable to accept constructive criticism.
- We are unable to give compliments.
- We find it difficult to express thanks.
- We have trouble admitting a mistake.

We all do these things from time to time. It is a problem when there's a pattern, when we use one or more avoidance methods often. Unfortunately, when looking at this list many of us would assure ourselves that we don't use such tactics at all. More false stories. These tactics keep us closed to the information we must have to move to inner peace. They seem to protect us from a lot of unpleasantness, especially in our relations with others. We do not like to be on the receiving end of these avoidances, but we often do not hesitate to use them on others. For many of us the avoidance methods may also indicate a fragile ego that is desperate for support. Unfortunately, a weak ego cannot be made stronger by external methods, and definitely not by any resort to certainty and avoidance of vulnerability. My ego definitely did not become stronger because I tried to maintain a picture of myself as invulnerable. I remained closed for decades, and suffered because of it.

It is not just because of fear of vulnerability or weak egos that we use such avoidances. We easily develop unpleasant habits of engaging with others, and often employ some of the avoidances. I once had a high-level manager as a client. He had an in-your-face style, one that was upsetting his staff. He demonstrated this style with some aggressiveness and at least two of avoidance methods, no apologies and no humility. When I asked him about that behavior, he saw nothing wrong in it. He told me that that was the way everyone in his family behaved, and they all did just fine—an unfortunate acquired habit which kept him in control, kept his world certain in his organizational work. He did not suffer much, but his staff did. He did not observe, or take action to improve, his adverse interactions with others, and thus caused diminished organizational effectiveness.

We can usually see that others are using some of the avoidances, but we often have no sense that we are using them. I had another client who told me that he was wide open to constructive criticism, that he had an open-door policy. Employees could come in at any time and tell him whatever they wanted. In his story he sincerely believed he was acting appropriately, even enthusiastically, when people provided difficult information. I surveyed his staff and found that his view, his story, was wrong. He was perceived as someone who would trash you, albeit politely, if you brought news he did not like or agree with. Whatever he heard that he did not like had to be eliminated. He had to be right, and he was certain that he was right. He was not consciously aware of his negative actions and thereby shielded himself from valuable information from his staff.

In her excellent book, *Passages*, Gail Sheehy says, "Growth demands a temporary surrender of security." Feeling vulnerable is natural when looking at our false stories and our attachments. There is considerable discomfort in facing those, but that uncomfortable sense is itself part of the path to inner peace, and is unavoidable. Can we open ourselves enough to surrender security? That is the question all seekers of inner peace have to ask. If the answer is yes, no matter what the pain or discomfort, then progress is possible. I use Chapter 3 to help those seeking inner peace understand and deal with this necessary discomfort.

The need to be certain does not get activated only when there is someone with whom we disagree. We can simply express every opinion, view, idea, any thought with firmness and absoluteness. We try to create the impression that there is no brooking our position on anything.

My wife and I made a friend shortly after we moved to the southwest. He is bright, pleasant, and often funny and expresses himself with absolute certainty on any topic. He talks constantly, and if someone else gets a word in, his certainty and authoritative power of expression ensure he gets the floor and the attention back. His need for certainty is so high that I have never heard him ask a question, except those with a sarcastic tone.

People in the grip of certainty often express themselves with considerable energy, which they describe as their passion showing. Passion for such folks is an unalloyed good, meaning that anything they say and how they say it is perfectly fine because it is driven by their passion. Unfortunately, while passion can be used for good, it can also be used for ill, such as overwhelming everyone else in the discussion. Using passion as a justification for our certainty behavior will benefit no one. We "think" we benefit because we feel a little boost when we project certainty. Sadly, this is temporary and impedes our movement to inner peace.

Related to vulnerability is self-consciousness. In the early stages of seeking inner peace we must allow ourselves to become acutely self-conscious. We will not know for sure what we are doing, and will be rather awkward in our practice of moving to inner peace. This is the same type of self-consciousness that we all experience when we are attempting to learn anything new. Until the new physical, mental or emotional changes become automatic, we exist in self-consciousness, an uncomfortable but necessary state which is the subject of Chapter 3. There is no escape from this in moving to inner peace. People needing to be certain find self-consciousness to be nearly intolerable because it detracts from the stories they have told themselves and is thus very threatening.

Our need to be certain and to appear invulnerable are like tyrants dictating behavior that causes us and others suffering. Many years ago I taught management at a community college. I told myself that I was very sensitive to student needs. In class one day a student politely suggested a view different from mine on a subject under discussion. I had an immediate defensive reaction and in no uncertain terms made sure the student was "corrected," shown the error of her ways. I was totally unconcerned whether she was factually correct or not (I later rationalized to myself why she was wrong, saving my own self-image, at least for a while). My concern was singular: get back in control, express certainty, and reinforce invulnerability. Make sure she and the rest of the class knew that I was in charge, in control. And my actions and their motives were totally unconscious to me. Hardly the makings of good teacher/student relations.

Mark Twain once said, "It ain't what you don't know that gets you into trouble. It's what you know for sure that just ain't so." This highlights a particular danger of certainty, knowing for sure what is not so. This attitude can cause large problems, especially when we make decisions about relationships, investments, jobs, and the like from a position of certainty.

It is a false story to which we are attached, and it compromises us and our relations with others.

But even if in our certainty we are factually correct, large difficulties arise because the problem is not whether we are correct or not. It is the need for certainty that obstructs our path to inner peace because it keeps us from the truth about our attachments and our problematic behaviors. When we are certain we see no reason, perhaps even have an aversion, to examining our inner selves and the quality of our connections with others. Certainty literally says we are correct in whatever we think, do or feel, about anything. This is another unfortunate false story, and information that contradicts it cannot be permitted. Uncertainty and vulnerability are part of getting to inner peace. In the introduction to Pema Chodron's (a Buddhist nun) lovely book, *Comfortable with Uncertainty*, Emily Hilburn Sell makes a wonderful observation: "What we call uncertainty is actually the open quality of any given moment." Can we face this with eyes wide open?

Our need to be certain and be in control is an understandable one, but in the end it offers no inner peace, only a temporary and illusory respite from suffering. Our need for certainty and our desire to avoid vulnerability impede our movement to inner peace because they close us off from information that is of the utmost value in our development. Further, these needs and desires once again are futile efforts to have the world be what we want it to be.

The issues of certainty and the need to be in control, if not challenging enough, can be made worse by our own biology. We have a reaction known as a Threat Response, an evolutionarily important protective mechanism. When we perceive any threat, physical, emotional, or cognitive, our mind/ body system instantaneously acts to protect us. It does not matter whether the threat is a lion staring us in the face from 5 feet, or the presence of a person whose views we do not like. Both are perceived by many of us as a threat, automatically engaging the Threat Response, which has two important elements.

In the first we restrict the flow of information and in the second we attempt to increase control. The goal of both is to get rid of the threat, and they occur immediately and unconsciously. In the jungle such a response is life-saving. In everyday life when we bump up against others or events that challenge us, it is a prescription for suffering. By narrowing the range of information that is allowed in we obstruct our movement to inner peace, which calls for the opposite—an unrestricted openness. By seeking control of others, we may assist them in activating their own Threat Response. The response actions are evolutionarily old and valuable. But when we are engaging with others, particularly when we are in conflict with them, the response actions are almost always inappropriate.

When acting from the Threat Response we are generally not aware of our actions. You have a view different from mine and my Threat Response kicks in creating the "must have" outcome that I want. Readers will see the connection of the Threat Response to certainty, to having our way unconditionally. It keeps us safe and restores order and control.

Because the Threat Response is built into our biology does not mean we have no choice in how we deal with any perceived threat. We can short-circuit inappropriate behavior through the on-going discipline of practice. The challenge is that the threat responses occur instantaneously and unconsciously. We do not think, "Well, that person's views are upsetting. I think I will activate my Threat Response and trash him." The response is out there long before we have any conscious recognition of what happened. The Threat Response system does not see the difference between the lion and the fellow whose views we despise, and it acts the same in each case.

People in long-term family, friend or romantic relationships often find their unpleasant responses to the other party have become "institutionalized." The behaviors have been acted out so often that they have become monumental habits, and are exceedingly difficult to change. A couple I know has been in this situation for decades. Every time she mentions something to him that he does not like, he mentions something she has done wrong. The original issues never get resolved, and the suffering continues.

The automatic nature of our problematic reactions means that we will be unable to stop those reactions until we reside for the most part in the present moment. As I mention in the Introduction, movement to inner peace requires that we monitor our thoughts, emotions, and actions. We can only do this if we exist in the present moment. The monitoring, coupled with subsequent control of our behavior, is how we ensure inappropriate actions are diminished or avoided, and how we move to inner peace and to being a force for good. We must constantly practice control in all the challenges, large and small, that life presents to us. This continuing work is of inestimable value in developing our monitoring awareness and control of behavior. Inner peace cannot be attained without it.

I have talked about the numerous ways our need for certainty and control causes both us and others problems. Those actions increase suffering and shield us from the information we most need in our search for inner peace, which requires that we accept and embrace uncertainty, vulnerability, and self-consciousness. If we cannot temporarily surrender our need for security, we cannot make progress in our search for inner peace.

CHAPTER 3

The Disorder of Learning

We learned in the last chapter why certainty and the fear of both vulnerability and self-consciousness block us from acquiring the information we need to develop inner peace and to connect well with others. While knowledge is needed for moving to inner peace, by itself it is insufficient. Learning entails both gains in knowledge and changes in behavior that result from that knowledge. The former without the latter may be interesting and beneficial if you live in a closet, but otherwise there can be trouble. In my life as a consultant I trained and coached many people in new organizational techniques and new behavioral dynamics—new knowledge. The trouble arose when this new knowledge was not translated into new behavior back in the work setting, meaning that my client wasted money and his people's time. Clients are very well-intentioned, but moving people to new behaviors, no matter how well they know what is needed and why, is very difficult under the best of conditions.

I think most seekers of inner peace are well-intentioned, just as my organizational clients were and just as I think I was. But neither my clients nor I was able to apply the understanding we gained from new knowledge, and I think this is true for many of us. Over 35 years ago I began avidly reading books on eastern philosophy and thought, and have read dozens of wonderful books filled with wisdom. For most of that time I learned nothing. Oh, I certainly acquired knowledge and had a wonderful emotional connection with the writers and their material, but I saw no connection between the important meaning in those books and my own behavior. I implemented nothing of benefit to me or others. But I sure enjoyed the reading, which provided me the excuse (although at the time I would have denied this vigorously) of avoiding the hard work of implementing the new knowledge.

For those of us seeking greater inner peace, the initial behavior change is often profoundly difficult. Opening ourselves to the falseness of our stories, to the damage of our attachments, to the harm we do to others, to seeing ourselves anew, can be shocking and painful. But this is the old view of ourselves, and it must be "destroyed" to make way for the new. This view has been around for a long time and is an intimate part of us which we have little desire to see disappear. Yet that is exactly what must happen, endlessly.

Shiva is one of the three great gods in Hinduism, and in the Dancing Shiva form both creation and destruction are present. The idea that creation requires destruction is a paradox many in the West are uncomfortable with. But like it or not, the reality is that old thoughts, views, assumptions, and stories must come to an end before we can become what we wish, before we can develop inner peace. Charles DuBois, a Belgian Naturalist of the 19th century said, "The important thing is this: to be able at any moment to sacrifice what we are for what we could become." To the degree that it impedes us, the old view must be sacrificed on the path to inner peace.

Even after acquiring new knowledge, however, we still face the daunting effort required to make actual movements toward inner peace. To gain inner peace we must alter ourselves internally through disciplined conscious effort that is done in conjunction with improving our relations with others.

Curiosity and mental and emotional openness are critical to seeking inner peace. They permit us to take chances with our mental states and emotions, to be vulnerable. In line with this is a quote from Shunryu Suzuki's wonderful book, *Zen Mind, Beginner's Mind,* "In the beginner's mind there are many possibilities, but in the expert's there are few." In searching for inner peace we have to become beginners again, and stay with a beginner's open and curious view of the world, forever. We must understand anew what it means to learn.

As we overcome our fear of the loss of control and give up our attachments, we open ourselves to the world and what it can teach us. Beginners again, we start the trek to inner peace. Many of us have read, some of us many times, the wonderful Zen proverb: When the student is ready, the teacher will appear. The "teacher" can be anyone or anything. An event, a person, a group, an emotion, an experience, or a series of these.

What triggers our positive response to such things? I don't think anyone knows. But as the proverb says, the student must be "ready." That may be a moment when we briefly let our guard down and allow in a bit of light. As Jung said, "One does not become enlightened by imagining figures of light, but by making the darkness conscious."

How did I get to "ready"? How did some of my darkness become conscious? I have examined my own "teacher," and realized it was for the most part not one person or one thing or one event. It was an accumulation, and all the books I had read were certainly a factor. But two things seemed to be part of the crystallization, and they happened more or less around the same time. The first was that I recognized that I was not totally happy with my relationship with my wife or with her daughters, and the feelings were mutual. I also saw that my connection with some of my closer friends was not very satisfying. I wanted all these relationships to be better.

The second "teacher" was my one moment of instant understanding. I had just finished reading the Dalai Lama's terrific book, *The Art of Happiness*. I was out walking and was suddenly struck forcefully by the fact that I had misunderstood, at a profound level, the nature of inner peace as the Dalai Lama explained it. I have read many of His Holiness's books, yet I never understood that the action of mental and emotional discipline was a big part of his view of inner peace. Additionally, I had defined mental and emotional discipline so narrowly that I missed their essence, all the while imagining that I understood those concepts and their application quite well.

The result of these two "teachers," but particularly the latter, was that I now knew what had to be done. For the first time I saw that I had to control my inner state and my behavior so that I became more emotionally healthy and a force for good for others. I had never even thought about this before, although I surely criticized others for their control failures. Perhaps an even bigger appreciation was that it no longer mattered whether others controlled their behavior or not. I could control only my own behavior and others would do what they needed to do. Gaining some level of inner peace seemed in part dependent on my treating others better, however they behaved.

In a way that I cannot fully explain, after decades I had reached some level of readiness. But I now began to appreciate how really hard it is to translate ideas about inner peace into action. I referred in the last chapter to both the challenge and the necessity of getting into the present moment so that we can monitor and control our behavior. My early attempts at this were not positive. I made more mistakes than I like to think about. But after some months I noticed that each moment of practice (required whenever I bumped into others or experienced unpleasant events) yielded a bit more inner peace. Still critical and judgmental, I had to work very hard to allow those undesirable emotions or behaviors to float away. Gradually I recognized in a visceral sense both the difficulty and the ultimate value of persistence.

Learning presents us with challenges at two stages. The first hurdle is our unwillingness to allow in information which upsets our view of ourselves. The second is the difficulty of implementing the information we do let in. These hurdles make it seem we are constantly in a state of imbalance, of disequilibrium, and to an extent that is true. But the learning process is more complex than that, and involves both equilibrium and disequilibrium.

At one level equilibrium is unquestionably needed. At another it seriously impedes movement to inner peace. It is positive when it is evidence of the lack of attachment, as in our having a balanced view of complex issue, or when we meet with equanimity an emotional challenge or upset. Balance can also be negative if it is associated with attachment to no change, to maintaining a permanent state of no growth, of certainty.

Our bodies need stability or we die. The body's intricate and beautifully balanced systems work to create and maintain equilibrium, or at least to keep most processes within very narrow ranges. We do not want our temperature fluctuating from 95 to 105 degrees. We do not want our pancreas secreting insulin at odd times for no reasons. We do not want our heart beating 60 times a minute and then 180 the next minute when all we are doing is watching not-very-exciting TV. Equilibrium is thus vitally important for our bodies' wellbeing.

But growth does not occur in equilibrium. Your muscles will not become more powerful if you sit in a chair and think about getting stronger. You will not become a good skier by reading winter wonderland magazines. The body has to be stressed for it to grow or develop new physical skills and capabilities. Of course, we can stress our bodies too much. But gradual and incremental stressing allows us to improve or learn new skills. For our body to grow it has to be thrown temporarily out of equilibrium. This does not mean that all bodily systems are stressed and out of equilibrium. Only some systems are stressed, and those in a careful manner.

We can apply the same thinking to how we learn cognitively. We cannot learn to speak Spanish, to repair a car, or to write short stories without pushing our mental systems off balance. When learning a new language, for example, we experience frustration and difficulty in making progress. And our communication effectiveness is compromised considerably, especially if the teacher insists that we use only Spanish in class.

Moving to inner peace requires that our minds and our emotions grow. We can look at that in the same way we would look at becoming a better skier or learning Spanish. We cannot evolve to inner peace without pushing our thinking and emotions into disequilibrium, out of balance, just as we cannot become a better skier without challenging our bodies in new ways.

We have all experienced the anxiety and frustration that physical and mental learning entails. But the challenges of emotional learning, which must happen in the movement to inner peace, are much greater. Why do we experience such a high level of difficulty in the search for inner peace?

Simply, we have more to lose. Perhaps we haven't learned Spanish very well or we are unable to grasp the intricacies of using our computer they way a 10-year old does. That may be embarrassing, but not much more. We may think that doing poorly in these two areas is not really about us at a deep personal level, but when we start talking about the inner us, now we are in dangerous and threatening territory. No longer is it merely about some competence we have or don't have. Now it is about who and what we are, and very few people want to go there. We have lived with our emotional setup (the stories and attachments) for a long while, and we cannot conceive of our emotional package being poorly developed and detrimental to us and others.

It is important to distinguish between an intellectual appreciation of inner peace and what it actually takes to bring about the new behavior. As we have seen, people can acquire knowledge and yet not change their behavior. I am a "terrific" example of that. Many of us, well-intentioned though we are, confuse inputs with outputs in trying to get to inner peace. We imagine that going to hear a person of great wisdom or reading one of the Dalai Lama's excellent books is how we acquire inner peace. A possible unconscious story is that these inputs by themselves will provide us with inner peace. We may be attached to the inputs and see those as the be-all and end-all of the process. Even if we acquire great knowledge from the inputs, there may be no motive to apply what we have received. Perhaps we intuitively know how very difficult that process is. Or, perhaps we are attached to our existing way of life, no matter what we say about developing greater inner peace. Or, perhaps our story that the inputs will produce inner peace is sufficient.

In order see how challenging real learning is, we need to look at the learning process. The generalized model below represents my conception of how people learn.

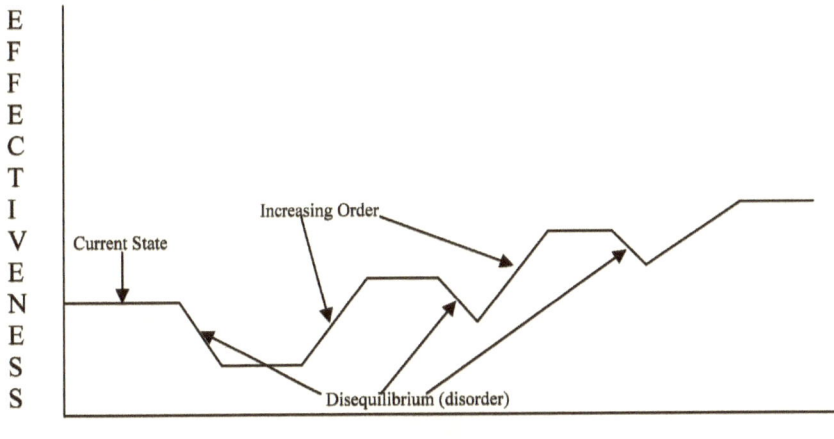

I cannot recall where I got this graph, but I used it originally in consulting with organizations whose new strategies or efficiencies required changed behavior throughout the organization. But the graph and what it stands for have a much broader application. The graph illustrates how we learn anything, from a physical skill to playing bridge to controlling our behavior to developing inner peace. It also shows that whatever we are learning requires that we struggle through the same dynamics of order and disorder to reach new levels of effectiveness, however that is defined.

As contradictory as this may sound, disorder is required to produce the order of greater effectiveness. Our effort to learn something starts from our current state, which is one of equilibrium, or order, and which can be zero for some things. Learning requires the acquisition of new information. Absorbing and attempting to apply the new information produces a period of disequilibrium, or disorder. Lowered effectiveness that is generally temporary (assuming we do not bail out prematurely) nearly always occurs, and this is normal. This period of disorder is often filled with anxiety and frustration because the new way of doing something pushes us so far out of equilibrium that we may feel like giving up. Naturally during this time we are likely to be quite self-conscious and experience vulnerability.

We are all familiar with the way a child learns to ride a bicycle. She has been riding a trike with considerable effectiveness and now we decide she is ready to learn how to ride a bicycle. We help her learn about the balance required for riding a bicycle and send her on her way. Naturally, she falls a lot. She has been removed from the orderly world of the trike and placed in the disorderly world of the bike. Her transportation effectiveness has diminished. But children, unlike many adults, don't give up. She continues to practice. Her effectiveness starts to increase as she falls less and soon becomes as comfortable riding her bike as she was riding her trike. Children have a determination that we must emulate. Progress toward inner peace requires a commitment to practice constantly and endlessly. We will "fall" a lot. That is part of the process. In fact, that is the process.

If we are committed to new learning, more effort is applied and through continued practice we begin to acquire new skills or get better at existing ones. The on-going practice is critical because we may temporarily forget the new learning and revert to past practice. Nevertheless, if we stick to it, our competence gradually increases. Order in the form of higher competence arises out of the disorder of disequilibrium. Learning without disorder and disequilibrium is not possible. The amount of physical, intellectual or emotional disorder is different for everyone, as is the way such disorder manifests in each of us. Some of us have a higher level of tolerance for ambiguity and uncertainty than others.

Even as we become more and more effective, we are still likely to experience setbacks and reversals, although the discomfort may be less and may last a shorter time. When my wife and I started learning tango, an extremely difficult dance to do well, we became extremely frustrated with each other. I believed mistakes were her fault. She obviously could not follow my leads. She believed mistakes were my fault. I obviously did not know how to execute a successful lead. We constantly argued about who was at fault for our many mistakes. We were in serious, and often hostile, disequilibrium for a number of years. The hostility over our dancing errors usually went unresolved and began to leak into other aspects of our relationship. To get our relationship back on track, we actually gave up tango lessons for about a year. Our love of the dance and each other prevailed. We started tango lessons again, making a promise to each other that when something went wrong we would stop, ask each other what we thought happened and try the move again, rather than immediately becoming judgmental, accusatory or irritated with each other. Practicing the new interactions proved very difficult and we made many mistakes just applying the new engagement rules. But order did arise out of this disorder and our tango effectiveness improved, as did the quality of our relationship.

Plateaus on the graph are stages where our new knowledge solidifies and becomes more accessible and usable. Our confidence expands and we are more willing to continue the growth process. These plateaus represent periods of relative equilibrium, where we can see we have achieved some level of increased effectiveness, a strong motivator. This could not be truer than in the search for inner peace, likely demanding the hardest effort of our lives. Our smallest gains are very important, and are to be cherished, but not clutched. Being out of equilibrium creates additional stress and frustration for all of us, and is especially challenging for those of us already having a great need for certainty, for stability. Unlike other learning, such as acquiring a new language, the learning involved with inner peace is particularly demanding because it involves devastatingly honest introspection, questioning our behavior and beliefs, and developing new ways of being. Persistence and commitment are required because movement toward inner peace is often slow and can take a long time.

During our inner peace search, how much our effectiveness is compromised and how long we spend in states of disequilibrium depend on the difficulty of the task; our openness; our abilities, drive and perseverance; and the amount of stress we experience. We may abort the process because the frustration, anxiety, disappointment and discouragement create more stress than we are able or willing to sustain. Sadly, in the search for inner peace the temptations to abort are high as we often unconsciously resist that which we say we want.

Order and disorder are not separate aspects of the world with no connection to each other. One without the other makes as much sense as talking about full and having no word for empty. Greater effectiveness in our emotional and spiritual lives is not possible without disorder and disorientation. As Chuang Tzu said,

"Consequently: He who wants to have right without wrong, order without disorder, does not understand the principles of heaven and earth. He does not understand how things hang together."

My quest to understand how things hang together required me to look deeply into myself, to face disorder, disorientation and disequilibrium. It has not been easy. To grow toward inner peace, I had to experience exactly what I wished to avoid, the challenges and disorientation of learning, a process that will continue forever. We are constantly bombarded with problem events and problem people, and we must be able to deal well with all of them. I work at this daily: at the market, while driving, in interactions friends and family. All of these are daily learning experiences, events that challenge me to practice and to continue to grow toward greater inner peace.

Everyone's growth demands disequilibrium and disorder. No one is immune, and growth requires that we give up our attachments to certainty and invulnerability. As sincere seekers of inner peace we must recognize that attempting to maintain our treasured state of equilibrium compromises our learning, our movement toward inner peace. We must move beyond the fear and open ourselves to learning, to putting into action what we now understand about the path to inner peace. So long as we hold onto our stories and attachments we cannot make much progress.

Moving toward inner peace requires that we look at aspects of ourselves and our behavior that may be very unpleasant. Earlier in the book I presented some of my false stories and concepts and the undesirable outcomes of those, evidence of my not being in a state of inner peace. Much of our effort to move to inner peace is dedicated to internal changes. But even gaining a level of inner peace through such efforts leaves something important yet to be learned, and this relates to our connection with others.

With inner peace we remain balanced when confronted by adverse circumstances or difficult people. Although inner peace is needed in both cases, the latter present a very different challenge from the former. Handling an unpleasant situation, such as our car's battery failing at the worst possible moment, is one thing. Responding from inner peace is all that is generally needed in this situation. Having a difficult interaction with another person is another thing. We wish to maintain our state of equanimity and respond in ways that are respectful of the other and uplift both of us. Doing this successfully requires that we acquire new understandings and new skills. We need to learn how to "manage" challenging interactions for the wellbeing of all, the subject of Ch 7.

Not all interactions are troubling ones. But many produce conflict, or disagreement. Conflict is neither good nor bad, but can be made one or the other by how it is carried out. Once we have inner peace, we can negotiate a challenging interaction, even one characterized by considerable negative conflict. For the most part what people want to argue or complain about is of minor importance. I recall with some embarrassment a small conflict between my wife and me (I say small and it was, but it was like most of our disagreements—of almost no import, but the stakes were high with both of us needing to win). I like language to be used crisply, not elastically, and the word "ready" when we are going somewhere has the meaning of "being at the door or in the car." I would ask my wife if she was ready and she would say yes nearly every time. I would go to the door only to realize my wife was still busy with something. This irritated me no end. Could she not possibly understand the meaning of a simple word! Many unpleasant interactions were occasioned by this little gem. We each failed to understand the other's use of language. I could not see that in my wife's view the word "ready" had a number of meanings, depending on the situation. Not wrong, just different.

As I came to understand and apply a bit of inner peace to challenging conversations, and to allow compassion to surface, I significantly altered how I interacted with others. I realized that very few situations called for me to differ actively and directly with anyone, no matter how much they wanted to differ with me. In fact, by becoming softer and more careful I have been able to aid both myself and others to move from a place of contest to one with more care and gentleness. Lao Tzu once said, "Softness triumphs over hardness," and "Nothing in the world is as soft as water, yet it can wear away the hardest of things." I do not mean I seek to triumph over anyone in challenging conversations. But my success in aiding myself and others to more helpful outcomes is made easier if I adopt softness, even if they are in a hardness or confrontational attitude. I had to relearn (really learn for the first time) how to bring respect and compassion to difficult conversations.

Learning is the key to gaining inner peace and to becoming a force for good. There can be enormous difficulty in acquiring often unpleasant information about ourselves and even more in applying it, and the desire to abort the effort is very strong at times. The journey to inner peace demands persistence and practice at levels we often cannot even imagine. We must take the empty-handed leap, and accept at our most visceral level that we can do it. Gradually, as we progress to inner peace new horizons open. No longer preoccupied with our own development (although we can never take that for granted), we can truly become active agents for good.

CHAPTER 4

Nothing Lasts

The Buddha spoke of impermanence, that nothing lasts, and that failing to understand the real nature of impermanence means suffering. Most of us would agree that impermanence, or change, is a fact of life. If I ask if the weather, a river, or a mountain will always be the same, most will say no. If I ask if we as individuals will never change, again most will say no. But here is the rub. Our sensitivity to impermanence shows up in our attachments to wishing for the world to be other than it is, unchanging. We exist in a conflicted state where intellectually we understand that everything changes, and all things good or bad pass away, but emotionally we hold onto the things we like and push away the things we do not like. This creates suffering as we are buffeted back and forth by the winds of change, experiencing emotional turmoil as we try mightily to hold onto this and get rid of that, all to no avail.

Change upsets us on a number of levels, one of which is the Buddha's profound existential challenge that we and all things are transient. Another is the pace and magnitude of societal change. And a third is the one that often gives us the most difficulty because of its frequency, our everyday bumps against reality. When we get attached to expectations about how the world should work and it does not conform to those expectations, we upset ourselves and we suffer. We try to resist what is. Common everyday dislocations include things like a condescending waiter, a person who nearly knocks us off the sidewalk, a letter from our credit card company asking what happened to our payment, or coming home from a trip to a swimming pool filled with algae (a personal "favorite" of mine which disturbs my equilibrium if I am not very careful).

Regrettably I have many examples illustrating my attempts to hold change at bay, to keep things as I wanted them. Years ago as a faculty member at a community college I was asked by my boss to work with a colleague on a project. I had very clear and certain ideas about how the project should go and what the outcomes should be, and I was quite firm on those. Unfortunately, my colleague's firmness and certainty equaled mine, and thus she represented a distinctly unwelcome intrusion into my orderly planning. The project turned into a very large contest of wills, each of us resisting the other. I saw her ideas as a repudiation of mine, and that simply could not happen. She saw things similarly. We resisted each other until we at last saw that we were in danger of creating an unsightly mess of the project. Neither of us thought we were wrong. Each of us was sure the other was wrong, but to keep the project from falling apart we had to cooperate, albeit grudgingly. Although the project was completed, both of us had acted badly and caused each other considerable difficulty. We had exported our lack of inner peace, evidenced by our needs to have the world as we wanted it.

Trying to create a world that it is regular and conforms to our wishes is futile, but that does not mean we cannot structure parts of our lives so there is some degree of regularity. How we drive home from work, what time we eat dinner, the restaurants we choose to patronize, how we keep our homes are all examples of small elements over which we have control and which can be healthy ways to deal with increasing change. The danger is getting attached to these "rituals," attempting to use them as a way to buffer us from having to deal with change in a direct manner, one intended to move us closer to inner peace.

Comforting as our "rituals" may be, nearly all change is outside our control. We control (at least are capable of controlling) only our emotions, thoughts and actions, but that is everything in the search for inner peace. But this "control" is unique and quite different from the normal use the word, which often seen literally. Control at this level is about maintaining something at a certain point or within a certain range, as with our heart rate, which cannot vary too much without killing us. There are many areas of life where literal control works perfectly, such as controlling our car, the amount and flow of information at work, or the shape of a bonsai plant. Unfortunately, this more literal concept of control often moves into problematic areas, such as the need to control others. As we have seen, this does not produce control but does produce suffering.

Control at the more subtle level is about change, as when we seek to control (change) our behavior so that we gain inner peace and become a force for good, and then to maintain that very desirable state. Paradoxically, I am talking about control by the absence of control. We generate an outcome such as improved behavior not through grabbing hold of it and forcing it to do as we want. We generate the new behavior by persistent mental and emotional discipline, and by allowing it to evolve with our permission, even while experiencing the natural frustration and anxiety of change. Exercising literal control (forcing) could push us into a "must have" state, which we know hurts progress toward inner peace. Putting effort into our discipline work and accepting the outcomes is control without control—the continued effort to produce emotional and mental discipline without attachment.

There is change that happens and there is change that we initiate. That which happens is beyond our control, although we may be able to act on it to some degree. We have already seen that attempting to keep at bay changes we do not like, and clutching onto those we do like, is of no avail. Progress toward inner peace asks for acceptance of change, but what does that mean?

We may think of acceptance as passivity, defeatism, or victimhood. It is none of those, but it is the beginning of the path to inner peace. In Buddhism acceptance is seen as a very powerful state, one that says, "I now see. I understand the true nature of the world." This form of acceptance allows us to engage the world of impermanence with equanimity and move toward inner peace. The power comes from understanding at both the intellectual and emotional levels that because nothing lasts there is nothing to get upset about, and that neither clinging nor pushing away will help us. It also comes from knowing we will decide our reactions, including what to feel, whether or not to act, and how to act. Our reaction will not be decided by the change, but by ourselves unencumbered by the need to fix the change or deny its existence. It is this freedom that allows us to settle into equanimity.

Acceptance does not mean we never take action when changes happen. Action is fine so long as we do not become attached to the effort or the intended outcome. We are often faced with changes that impact us for good or ill, and action can often be of great value. Consider that we have been diagnosed with a serious disease. We have a natural desire to take action to stem or eliminate the bodily threat. Acceptance means we undertake action without the expectation that we "must have" our outcome. Can we hope for a positive change in the body? Of course. It is only the attachment to the outcomes of the treatment that can cause suffering.

While action is often appropriate, action for action's sake will not help. The societal turmoil today may push people into an I-have-to-do-something frame. Pema Chodron has written,

> "We become habituated to reaching for something to ease the edginess of the moment. Thus we become less and less able to reside with even the most fleeting uneasiness or discomfort." (*Comfortable with Uncertainty*)

The turmoil and speed of change can easily result in our feeling lots of edgy, stressful moments, and the daily obstructions of life add considerably to our discomfort when our plans and expectations are disrupted. But it is not just these that cause us trouble in the search for inner peace. The challenge of progress is made even tougher because we have grown used to not being bored, to being constantly stimulated. A moment without action, noise, music, internet-searching, or social-networking may produce anxiety, and thus tempt us to remove the anxiety. The idea that a moment of nothing, of silence, can be beneficial is often not recognized. So we have a double-whammy paradox: change can produce fear and anxiety, and the lack of change (such as momentary silence or non-action) may also produce fear and anxiety. In the grip of such internal conflict we cannot move very easily toward inner peace.

Our life is filled with changes that come out of the blue, unanticipated. The car breaks down, people on our cruise ship come down with a severe virus, the company is closing its office in our city, our ten-year old breaks an arm in a football game, or among the worst of all, our spouse dies. Such changes may be awkward at best and truly debilitating at worst. Acceptance allows us to healthily absorb the challenges with equanimity. This is not to say that people with inner peace never experience physical or emotional pain from certain changes. It is that they do not become enmeshed in wishing for things to be different than they are. Thus, the pain, severely emotional in the case of the death of a spouse, does not become suffering.

The fast change and uncertainty of today's world, along with the disturbances of daily life, may lead us to fret about things that might happen. When we worry about the future we are not in the present moment. We lodge our thinking and emotions in a possible future, usually threatening, and then upset ourselves about what might happen, working the suffering like grinding on a bad tooth. A friend is disturbed over the loss of physical attractiveness as she ages, and this causes her to suffer. But even more challenging, and producing more suffering, is that she worries over future physical changes. The Dalai Lama has addressed worry when he said if there is a solution, why worry, and if there is no solution, why worry. I would add that if you are not sure if there is a solution, why worry. This is acceptance, and inner peace.

I have spoken mainly about negative change, but positive change does happen, such as winning a horse race, being nominated for a special award, or discovering that we have a talent for music. These are often far fewer than the changes that cause us problems, but they can be just as debilitating if we become attached to them, if we expect that only good changes will happen or that the good experiences we have must stay

Most of us know that change can easily generate resistance, which is the effort to get the bad event or situation to pass away or the good to stay as we see it disappearing. We resist the world as it is and try to create one that is not real but which makes us "happy." We have all experienced resistance to change in one way or another. I recall an amusing (now, not then) interaction with one of my boys who was six months old. I was feeding him mashed vegetable and he spit out the spoonful all over me. Resistance starts early.

Sadly, the more effort we apply to making the world unchanging, to resisting what is, the more suffering we experience because the world goes on its merry way whether we like it or not. In our strong need to escape the change, we are like an animal caught in a net. The animal thrashes with increasing desperation in an effort to escape, only making the net tighter. Or think about going to get a shot at the doctor's. Resistance, or tightening one's muscles in anticipation of pain, causes the pain of the shot to be worse. We can resist what is, but there is a cost to us and often to others. Recall my earlier example of the college project I worked on. Both my colleague and I resisted each other and that cost each of us anxiety and frustration, a loss of energy that could have gone toward the benefit of the project. The fact that we managed to finish the project does not justify our behavior toward each other.

One of the ways we try to deny impermanence, to resist change, is expressed by Matthieu Ricard in his superb book, *Happiness*: "When we look outward, we solidify the world by projecting onto it attributes that are in no way inherent to it . . . . We spontaneously assign intrinsic qualities to things and people, thinking 'this is beautiful, that is ugly,' without realizing that our mind superimposes these attributes upon what we perceive." By assigning arbitrary qualities to things, people, or events we construct a false reality, one to which we may be attached and one which must be defended as though it were real. We are trying to solidify our world, to make it real and unchangeable and to provide us the security of certainty.

While resistance to change seems unhealthy and a barrier to inner peace, we come by some of our resistance to change naturally. As I mentioned earlier, evolution has "created" the Threat Response as a way to protect us from serious danger, which was plentiful in the long past and which usually manifested by some change in the environment. Generally speaking, in evolutionary terms any change in our environment was more likely to be harmful than to be beneficial. So we respond to change warily, but being wary is not always the same as resistance, although our natural wariness can easily translate into outright resistance when we feel threatened by change, as is often the case today.

A great deal of psychological work has been done on why we resist change. Each of us responds differently to change, and we activate our own unique form of resistance. Fear of the unknown, fear of failure, fear of loss, fear of upsetting others are only a few examples of what might drive any one of us to resist change. Resistance efforts are not the same as non-attached action we might take to address a change that we want to influence. In the former we "must have" a different outcome, and invest considerable effort and emotion into getting it. Not getting the new outcome produces suffering because, in simple terms, we want what we want and we can't have it. In the non-attached situation we may also want a different outcome, but we invest no emotion, no "must have" in the new outcome, even while putting effort into getting it. We accept the outcome, whatever it is.

Perhaps the most common activator of resistance is the actions (or non actions) of other people. We want people to act as we desire them to, not as they often do. We may see the actions of others as obstructions to our wellbeing, and just as often seek to control them. People do not like being controlled and they will activate their own resistance, making everything considerably worse. Sadly, controlling others often takes unpleasant and disrespectful forms. Consider anger, sarcasm, dismissive tones, sulking, victim-hood, or guilt, which represent only a few of the many ways we may try to manipulate others into doing what we want. Suffering for us and for them.

Our search for inner peace asks that we accept change, and one of the keys to this is being in the present moment. Being in the present moment allows us to stay with problematic thoughts, emotions and even actions, and not try to push them away. Being in the present moment allows us to understand fully what we are experiencing, and to "control" unhelpful reactions, particularly resistance. As with all problematic reactions, we can settle into equanimity more easily by acknowledging and accepting the reactions and not becoming attached to ridding ourselves of them. Being able to simply "be" with those reactions helps us on the path to inner peace because we give them no power to affect us, no hold on us. Simply observing and making no judgments about the reactions becomes the same as saying, "Ah, the wind is up." We have observed the wind and then we gently move our thoughts elsewhere. Inner peace is about observing but not hanging onto the reaction we have to, say, an irate client exactly the way we observe the wind. If we can do it for the wind, we can do it for the irate client, and for everything else. It all depends on practice, endless practice.

No matter how hard we try to maintain our current existence in the forms we most desire, we will fail. We will suffer and so will those around us. Trying to halt change is like trying to swim against the current of an enormous river. We will battle until we die and achieve nothing but suffering. But embracing change, whether coming from outside or inside of us, frees us from the need to swim in any direction except with the current.

Thus far I have talked about change that happens and how we must accept that in the Buddhist sense. Most of us also have goals for improving ourselves and our lives, self-initiated change, perhaps the most important of which is that of inner peace.

Henri Bergson, the French philosopher, once said: "To exist is to change, to change is to mature, to mature is to go on creating oneself endlessly." His idea fits well with all things being ephemeral. Inner peace is not a state at which we arrive and in which we live blissfully ever after. It is an on-going and never-ending process of growth and reconfiguration of our inner and outer lives. The choice we will all make is whether to allow outside forces or our possibly deluded inner selves to "create" us over and over in less desirable ways, or whether we will take command of our growth in a true act of continued recreation, each step of which moves us closer to inner peace.

Change that we actively seek, such as losing weight, learning aikido, developing better relationships, or becoming enlightened can produce fine and useful outcomes. It allows us some sense that our destiny is in our hands and not in the hands of forces beyond our control. These personal changes are admirable and healthy. The change goal of gaining greater inner peace is so important because the quality of our entire life will improve with each bit of progress. But, again, we must be alert to the danger of becoming attached to these goals, especially that of inner peace. The innate attractiveness of our positive goals can be very seductive. I have a friend who is very sincere about becoming enlightened. Unfortunately, he is attached to the idea of enlightenment and thus cannot see what really needs to be done to move in that direction. He recognizes he is not making progress, and that upsets him considerably, but it is not clear to him that he could make progress if he gave up the need to make progress, if he lost his attachment.

Most of us know at least intuitively that not all change is created equal. The following quote from Irene Peter, an American epigrammatist, makes a wonderful connection: "Just because everything is different doesn't mean that anything has changed." Can something have changed and not changed? It depends on the level at which we examine the issue.

I once did consulting work for a large non-profit organization. I was hired to assist top management in reorganizing much of upper management so that operations would be more efficient. I developed a suggested structure, with managers changing positions, reporting requirements, and acquiring new titles. Top management implemented my ideas. I was called back about 6 months later and told that my ideas had not worked at all and to figure out why. Managers I interviewed told me that changes had been made at one level, the superficial one of who reported to whom and who had what title. But the changes needed at a deeper level, the ones that would produce greater efficiency, had not happened. Things looked different, but the way business was done had not changed. I misunderstood the level at which I should have been helping the organization. The superficial change had masked a deeper set of behavioral problems, and changing the former did nothing to address the latter. I fell into the trap of not being aware of the level of real change the organization was looking for and needed.

We can fall into a similar trap in our self-generated change, particularly that connected to inner peace. As I have said, we may pursue inner peace by reading books, meditating, or listening to wise masters, which is one level of looking for inner change. But if these efforts are not accompanied by hard work and discipline, the more demanding level of the search for inner peace, we will not move forward. The trap occurs when we mistake the level at which we need to be working, seeing one thing, the inputs, and actually looking for another, the outcome of real inner peace. We may think we are making progress toward inner peace, but mostly our efforts will result in the appearance of change and not the real thing. This illusion has its own cost.

A valuable way of looking at our healthy acceptance of and participation in change comes from systems theory, an interdisciplinary approach that studies mainly self-regulating systems, such as the human body, organizations, climate, and groups. This quote from Daniel Goleman's fine book, *Primal Leadership*, gets at a critical piece in our search for inner peace: "Systems theory tells us that in an environment of turbulent change and competition, the entity that can take in information most widely, learn from it most thoroughly, and respond most nimbly, creatively, and flexibly will be the most adaptive."

Although Goleman is addressing organizational functioning in the quote, his point applies to our personal movement to inner peace. His reference to turbulent change could easily apply to the turmoil of our world today, the product of faster and larger changes, heightened unpredictability, and an increased sense that we don't know what will hold us together in the midst of all this. Like adaptive organizations, we must be open to new and often disconcerting information, and to changing our behavior (adapting) as a result of this new information. Taking in information widely and responding flexibly, both internally and externally, are two critical elements in our own growth to inner peace. They are also very important in our becoming a force for good.

Flexible responses are important because change comes whether we like it or not and it usually presents a different face each time, which can create the uncertainty and unpredictability many of us desire to escape. Having adaptable responses which take into account the very different changes we are likely to experience means developing multiple ways of seeing, examining and dealing with any change, including internally-generated change. The fewer and less diversified our options, the more rigid our mind and responses may be. And conversely, the more rigid our mind, perhaps the more enmeshed in certainty, the fewer options we have. More options present a possibility of greater inner peace and for connecting compassionately with others.

We develop multiple options by wide-open information gathering, by restricting nothing and by avoiding attachment to the way we want the world to be. Certainty reduces the flow of information and thus minimizes the diversity of responses. Inner peace is aided by having multiple, often innovative, ways of dealing with the various challenges we all experience. My false story that anyone who disagreed with me was not very bright is an example of limited options. Since the story reigned supreme, my only actions when confronted with someone whose views differed from mine were to attack and castigate. As I made progress on the path to inner peace, I realized that not having to win, be right, or fulfill a false story gave me all sorts of options for how to deal with folks who had different views. As I tried being a force for good, I saw that simply disagreeing with someone was seldom useful or helpful, and produced predictable unpleasant outcomes. With no investment in the discussion that had to be defended, I realized I could constructively and respectfully interact with nearly anyone, no matter how far apart our views. The dialogues in Chapter 7 illustrate how to have quality discussions no matter how great our differences are.

There is an important sidelight to our attempts to make the world into what we want, and to keep it that way. As we try to keep change at bay, two things happen. One that I have already mentioned is that large amounts of energy are used in this futile effort, causing difficulty and suffering. The second is that the longer we strenuously resist what is, the greater the difficulty when we can no longer maintain the resistance and the issue has to be faced. Corrective action to get things back to "normal," assuming that is even possible, can be enormous.

As an example, some years ago I had a small community bank for a client. The bank had been in existence for about 2 years when the entire teller staff (8 women) quit simultaneously one Monday morning. The president was in shock, and asked me to find out what happened. It was actually quite simple. The VP of Operations supervised the tellers, whom he treated nastily. The President had heard rumors of this bad treatment but dismissed those because he "knew" the VP was a good man. This denial continued even though members of the community also made reference to "bank problems." The President avoided reality, maintaining a fiction instead, and paid a significant price. He saved the bank, but just barely, and had to prove to the small community that workers would be respected. Had he acted much earlier, the needed corrective action would not have been so large.

Another example dealt with a marriage I am familiar with in which the husband demeaned his wife in front of others, always with a smile as though his remarks and tone were only a joke. I could see that she did not find it humorous, but she apparently wanted to avoid conflict and never said anything to him. Her only "message" was a tightening of her lips and a little blush, signals he totally missed. After around 15 years of marriage, she simply disappeared, and the husband had no idea what happened. The wife went to her sister's house and never returned, divorcing her husband. As the wife described it, she had lived with this behavior for years and was storing more and more anger against him until finally she had had enough. The husband saw nothing wrong and continued his behavior. In the end he had no possible corrective action, no way to retrieve the marriage.

In both the bank and the marriage cases there was undesirable behavior that eventually led to an abrupt and very challenging situation. The bank president was fortunate enough to implement corrective action which saved the day, although the effort was substantial, and the bank's survival in doubt for a considerable time. The husband in the marriage scenario had no such possibility.

Accepting the inevitability of change is part of the path to inner peace. But perhaps even more important in moving to inner peace is accepting that change is also unavoidable. Nothing lasts, not good and not bad, and there is nothing we can do about that impermanence. Our resistance efforts to retain the good and push away the bad are futile. They provide us with only the momentary illusion of success, of keeping the change at bay. We have seen in the two examples above that denying what is happening before us is usually very costly. We may want everything to remain as is, but change is happening whether we see it or not. The bank President saw something, but took no action until it was nearly too late. The husband never saw anything, so no action was possible.

Our inability to have much of an impact on change means we are often beset with frustration and fear. Sadly, we not only share our negative emotions with others, we also share the suffering that accompanies that. Acceptance in the Buddha's sense is the only healthy way to "deal" with change. Where possible, action is fine, but it has to be taken with the view that the action may or may not make a difference, and we can live with that. Taking action and trying hard, often extremely hard, is not a problem until it becomes a "must have" outcome.

Change is. There is no avoiding, denying, or stopping it, only acceptance.

CHAPTER 5

Getting the Help We Need

There are two major aspects connecting our relationships with others to our search for inner peace. The first is that we cannot achieve a much improved level of inner peace without the help of others. The second is that their wellbeing is to some extent dependent on us. The better we behave (the more inner peace we have) the better our relationships with them become, thereby benefitting them. Compassion asks that we actively and positively take the wellbeing of others into account, and which I address in Chapter 7. This chapter is about seeking and applying the help we need and can get from others on our path to inner peace.

There are people who can achieve some level of inner peace by themselves, but they are very few. Most of us need the assistance of those who care for us. But given the intensely personal and challenging nature of moving on the path to inner peace, how can they assist us?

When we act out our false stories and concepts, causing ourselves and others problems, we cannot see what is really happening, why we are getting "strange" reactions from them. We often miss the signals telling us that others are not happy with our behavior. But this information, if we see it at all, is often interpreted as a problem with them, not with us. Trapped in this false view, the problem is "out there," and we continually experience frustration and suffering trying to fix it. Our behavioral problems are the overt manifestations of our lack of inner peace, and that is why those who care for us are so important in the path to inner peace. They often see what we cannot.

I have found that others can help us in two ways, one direct and one indirect. Both are based on the idea that we cannot see ourselves and our behavior very well at all, and what we do "see" is usually so biased in our favor, convoluted, and wrong that it has little value. But our false stories, attachments, emotional acting out, and irrational concepts are often visible to those around us, and that is the stuff of real value. In the direct approach people close to us can provide guidance and assistance in our search for inner development. It involves on-going, face-to-face communication and interaction with a helper who can see what we cannot.

In the indirect approach we carefully observe others' reactions to us, in any circumstance. Carefully and non-judgmentally observing these reactions, which are mainly non-verbal, gives us a huge amount of information about how we are perceived by those around us. We come across well in some settings, but I am concerned with when we come across badly, when we are out of the present moment and our attachments show up. The method is indirect because we do not directly engage others, but merely observe them and their reactions to us. It is useful for all seekers of inner peace, and particularly valuable for those without helpers at the moment. I will talk more about the indirect method below.

Unfortunately, when we ask people who know and care for us for direct input and help in seeing our own challenges, there can be problems. Even those closest to us are likely to be apprehensive about giving us the real story. They don't want us to be upset with them and they don't want to be harmed, both reasonable concerns. We can do a lot of damage when we are not in the present moment and in control of our behavior. The goal of asking for help is to get help, not to kill the messenger no matter how unpleasant the message or its delivery. To properly receive a challenging message, we must make every effort to be in the present moment, balanced and respectful. This is tough enough under reasonably good conditions, but is a real trick under the adverse conditions of receiving difficult personal information.

Another difficulty is communication problems arising from people's personalities or their unique communication styles, such as being direct or indirect, loquacious or terse, literal or figurative, big picture oriented or detail oriented. Further, there are people whose ability to get a thought across is compromised by their lack of clear thinking, or by a difficulty with language, or a problem with listening. For the seeker of inner peace these difficulties are not relevant. Whether the helper's style is one we can connect with or not, or whether the helper has no trouble or real trouble getting his point across—these matter not at all. Every helper will likely have some kind of communication difficulty, and even that is a golden opportunity for our practice.

Outright errors are a likely possibility, as when what the helper is providing is flawed or totally incorrect, possibly an outcome of his or her own challenged and unconscious world view. For example, I asked a friend for feedback on any behavior of mine that he considers troubling. He tells me that I do not communicate well, leaving people unclear about what I mean. Specifically, he says that I wander without focus. The challenge for me in this case is that he is actually talking more about himself than me. He sees me doing what he does, and is unconsciously projecting that defect onto me. I may have communication problems, but this isn't one of them. So what do I do? I certainly do not try to inform him of his error. Error problems like this can occur easily with our helpers, and we must still move forward. My solution was to thank him for his thoughts and try with questions to obtain more information about other aspects of my communication that are problematic.

Non-verbal communication can also cause problems. Somewhere around 75% or more of the meaning of all face-to-face communication is carried through everything other than the words themselves. There is body posture, tone of voice (and lots of other voice aspects, such as articulation, speed, etc.), facial expressions, and eye movements, to name some obvious ones. What people send non-verbally is what they really mean, no matter what the words say. In the midst of disagreements with my wife I have said, "Of course you are right, dear," accompanied by a big sigh and a downcast tone of voice. My wife knew immediately that the sigh and the tone were real and the words, even though positive, meant little. Any chance of a positive resolution of the issue went right out the window.

Some time back while on a short vacation a friend needed to get in touch with us, and left a bunch of messages on the home phone. As soon as we arrived home we called the friend, and he said, "Oh, THERE you are!" with a frustrated tone of voice and plenty of emphasis on THERE. The message my wife and I got was clear: what he was really saying was, "Where the hell have you been!!! How dare you not be there when I want you!!!" His comment and the emotion attached to it, expressed non-verbally, chastised us for our dereliction. I asked him later about his tone of voice and he could not imagine how we had gotten such a negative impression. He cannot see, and thus exports suffering.

We all have agendas, mainly stories, concepts, and attachments. But there is also anger and fear at deep levels we do not see, and these will be conveyed primarily non-verbally. For example, consider that a husband asks his wife to help him move toward inner peace, and she is happy to do so. Unfortunately, she is still angry at him for what she perceives as years of him cutting her off in conversations (another bit of problematic non-verbal behavior), something she is unaware of and thus has never brought up. She may control what she says (the words), but her unconscious anger, even if very subtle, will leak out non-verbally. And that is what the husband will interpret as real and react to, often with unpleasant results. Negative non-verbal cues absolutely trump positive words. The seeker must be able to allow any negativity to pass by and move forward.

Certainly not all non-verbal signals are negative. Many express fine things like love, joy, excitement, enthusiasm, and the like. My concern is not with these. It is with those non-verbal cues that cause our conversations to go to pieces in an instant, and obstruct our search for the information that will lead us closer to inner peace.

We have acquired a repertoire of non-verbal responses over the years we have been alive, and nearly all of those have been acquired unconsciously. We seldom know what we are sending, particularly when we are stressed, and we do not understand the often negative impact on others. Since we cannot see or appreciate what we are sending non-verbally, a negative reaction by another is perceived as something having to do with them, and not at all to do with us.

Notwithstanding the above challenges of connecting to our helper, the interactions we have and the information we get is highly beneficial! How can that be if the information is poorly delivered or is partly or totally wrong? Simple: the information, the way it is delivered, and the person helping us are all part of the path, no matter what the delivery sounds like or how wrong the helper's perception of us is. This is practice staring us right in the face. Wrong or badly delivered information still allows us to start the conversation and engage the helper with dedication and care no matter how difficult it is. And that is practice, and is invaluable. Because of the challenges of getting quality information, and of our difficulties in receiving it, we must be extremely wary of our own reactions, especially the non-verbal ones. As I said, it is tough enough to hear challenging information which is correct, but to hear information that is clearly wrong can be devastating. And we move forward regardless. For a true seeker after inner peace there is no other option.

A very important decision, then, is who to ask to be the helper (and there certainly can be more than one). Ideally this person should be someone who clearly cares for us and desires to assist us. The helper could be a relative, a spouse or life partner, a sibling, or a very good friend. A caution:

We should be prepared for that person to say no, and that is alright. When we ask someone to do something, we must give them the right to say no, without any recriminations. Seekers who have no one to use as a helper in the inner peace search can do work on their own.

How do we manage when there are all kinds of problems associated with getting the feedback we need? The biggest challenge I experienced in my search was managing my reactions to my helper's input. Behavioral control is likely to be weak when we are just getting started on the path to inner peace. True seekers of inner peace have to alter the game at the start with their helpers by ensuring that the latter know they will not be punished for their revelations. Many seekers will agree with the idea of no recriminations, but they have no idea of the subtle and unconsciously-driven negative responses they can give that will harm the helper and shut down a vital source of information. As with nearly everything related to moving into inner peace, being in the present moment while receiving challenging information is vital.

Recognizing that we have had no preparation for the inputs we are likely to get, jumping right in with our helper may not be the best idea. What can be done to prepare us for the interactions that will move us towards inner peace? The suggestions below are based on my own personal experience that led to my getting a bit closer to inner peace.

One early strategy is for us to practice on our own by imagining unpleasant news we might get from our helper. It should be unpleasant, even irritating. We can then imagine a dialogue in which our helper passes this information to us. We can experience feeling angry, resentful, or abused at the information or the way the information is provided. We can envision the conversation continuing to go badly, for any number of reasons, but particularly because the helper is upset and also wrong by our view. We allow, even encourage, our negative emotions to push us into inappropriate behavior.

With no threat since the whole thing is imagined, we can analyze our emotions and our behavior in the dialogue. We can focus especially on the words we used, our non-verbal messages, and what we were feeling. It is important that we do not beat ourselves up. We want to look at our reactions and responses and think about how well or poorly they served us in the conversation, and we want to do this analysis a number of times. It is also important that we go very slowly in replaying the dialogue and reviewing its results. When confronted with irritating information or behaviors from others, the tendency is to move very rapidly to get rid of the unpleasantness or attack the helper, reactions driven by negative emotions. Being slow in our examination helps avoid that reaction, and is expressed beautifully in this wonderful Thai proverb: "Life is short, so we must move very slowly."

The next step in working on our own is to replay the same conversation, this time visualizing ourselves dealing well with the negative emotions, not allowing them to influence our reaction to the news. We can let the dialogue play out, with us being totally in control of our emotional responses and our behavioral reactions, imagining the dialogue going extremely well. As with the dialogue that went badly, we analyze this one completely several times. We can review what we felt, what we did with those feelings, and how we ensured they did not affect our behavior. Did we listen carefully? Did we ask clarifying questions when needed? Did we act slowly and carefully throughout the conversation? Did we show respect for our helper in both words and actions? For maximum benefit we can replay this positive conversation again and again.

After doing our inner role play, a second strategy is to ask our helper to write down two or three problem aspects of our behavior. Ask that person to describe when each behavior is present and how it shows itself, including non-verbal aspects. We won't do anything with this written information until we have time to ourselves. Then, no matter how wrong we think the information is, we construct positive dialogues as above to deal with it. We work through these issues a number of times until we feel reasonably comfortable with our understanding of them and our reactions. This allows us to desensitize ourselves somewhat. While we are working through this process, we can identify the troubling behavior in each situation. Then, we need to practice again and again. Slowly.

After processing the problems described by our helper comes the very important third strategy—talking with our helper about those problems. Maintaining the best command of our behavior is vital, both the words and the non-verbal aspects. By now we know that we will make plenty of mistakes, with emotions often trying to crowd out calm and thoughtful responses. We must assure our helper that mistakes on our part have nothing to do with him/her, but are all about us and our need to achieve inner peace. We can describe to the helper what some of our mistakes might look like. No matter how badly the conversation actually goes, we strive to maintain our balance the best we are able. If the information we get is questionable or badly delivered, it is not helpful to try to "fix" (correct) the helper. Accept the person's mistakes and move on. As I have said, poor or badly delivered information is a wonderful occasion to practice. Try not to pass it up.

Below are two dialogues, one showing poor seeker behavior and the other useful seeker behavior.

> Seeker: What have you noticed about my behavior that you think is something I should look at? (gentle tone)
>
> Helper: Why do you always get SO sulky whenever I ask if you can help around the house? (whining, victim)
>
> Seeker: What are you talking about, I never sulk! Here I am trying to improve myself and all you can do is criticize me. (anger and defensiveness)
>
> Helper: Well, you asked me and now you're jumping down my throat. (victim)
>
> Seeker: What are you talking about! I'm hardly jumping down your throat! (anger, defensiveness)

The situation broke down almost immediately with the way the helper phrased the information. But that is the way things go, and they will go that way often. The real problem is how the seeker handled (really, didn't handle) the comments. How could this have gone better?

> Seeker: I don't want to give a sulky impression, so could you tell me what you hear and see that tells you I am being sulky? (Notice how the seeker avoids defending himself. Notice further that he also does not go after either the statement about "always" or the whine)
>
> Helper: Well, sometimes you have acted unhappy when I have asked you to help around the house. You get rather silent and I think I am getting punished for asking you.
>
> Seeker: Thank you for that input. Do you see any other signs that I am displeased with you?
>
> Helper: Yes, you sniff.
>
> Seeker: I'm sorry?
>
> Helper: You start sniffing. I only hear that when you're irritated, so I know you are upset.
>
> Seeker: I am totally unaware of doing that. Do I sniff in other settings, or just with you?
>
> Helper: I have only seen it with me. It makes me feel diminished.

The seeker in the first dialogue could not (chose not to) control his behavior, but in the second did an excellent job. I know the experience of being on the receiving end of information delivered badly, so I am aware that anyone in the same situation will likely feel negative emotions. The seeker in the first dialogue failed to control the expression of those emotions; he fell out of balance, out of being fully present. But in the second he did a fine job. He now has excellent information to begin changing his behavior as part of his path to inner peace. The last comment by the helper has to be dealt with as it indicates harm for her, and that means the conversation will have to go on, if not now, then later. Much more will come out as the seeker, by staying in control of his behavior, continues to provide the helper with an increasing sense of safety. Seekers need frequent feedback on how well they are doing in controlling behavior and changing adverse reactions to more positive ones, and this all takes time. And helpers need thanks and appreciation for their help.

In the second dialogue the seeker was very careful of how he related to the helper. There are some very important ideas that a seeker can use to help control behavior and ensure a positive direction for the conversations. After the seeker asks the helper for very specific input about his/her behavior, it is wise and very effective practice to:

- Ask questions that help clarify what the helper is saying.
- Make few if any statements, as we learn little from them.
- Avoid defending oneself (As in, "Let me tell you why you are wrong").
- Refrain from disagreeing with the helper, even if the latter is incorrect.
- Address only the issue being presented and no other.

These suggestions help ensure the conversation goes productively. They help the seeker in controlling emotional responses, and they also aid the helper in gaining greater clarity as the seeker asks questions. Beyond this, these suggestions are useful for nearly any conversation, particularly those in which there is conflict, a subject of Chapter 7. That chapter also has a variety of dialogues illustrating good and not-so-good behavior applicable in demanding interactions, whether those are with our helper or with anyone else.

While all of this work is going on with our helper (it could be months or more), we can practice with any situations that are upsetting, that move us from inner peace. The car in front cuts us off. The clerk at the store is rude. We wonder why the woman in line cannot stop talking and just pay for her groceries. We are repairing something at home and hit our finger with the hammer. Our child talks back to us. Our spouse fails to take get groceries. A colleague at work offers insulting remarks. The assistant at the hardware store talks condescendingly to us. The person at the end of the 800 line we called to get a credit card problem worked out seems unable to understand our issue. The laundry ruined one of our best shirts or blouses.

Each of these challenges elicits negative emotions, which create suffering and undermine our inner peace. We want them to go away! But this is the way life goes, with constant challenges to our inner peace. Each and every one of these challenges is like gold—a marvelous chance to practice equanimity. But, "Don't I have a right to be upset when I was spoken to rudely by someone?" Of course we do have that right, but why would we want to upset ourselves? If we allow such upsets to happen we are saying that our emotions and our reactions are under the control of some other person or event. Most people I know do not like that idea and for good reason—it is both a disturbing image and a prescription for suffering.

If we sincerely want inner peace, we must practice constantly, all day long as challenges arise, getting a handle on our emotions and actions, and not reacting when we bump up against the real world. Inner peace will start to show up when these events or thoughts no longer bring out unpleasant emotions to the extent they once did. And as inner peace increases, even when emotions arise they are allowed to float away easily and do not impact our thinking or acting. Practice is the key to everything, and the harder the situation or person challenging us the better. Such practice is closely connected to the work we do with our helper. As we respond more healthily to life's ups and downs in general, we will also become more able to take in and deal well with the often challenging information we get from our helper.

The negative reactions we experience throughout the day represent attachments to our need for problematic things and people to be gone, immediately. These reactions represent a judgmental view of the world, valuing this as good and that as bad. The outcome is suffering. We have all built up a juicy reservoir of things and people that upset us, and we are continually adding new ones. We naturally justify every one of these reactions, ensuring that the suffering we get with each incident will be even greater the next time around.

Controlling our emotions and responses is very difficult, and we cannot use our usual fruitless method of forcing our emotions to do what we want. As I mentioned in earlier chapters, a very helpful approach when problematic thoughts or emotions arise is to accept them, note their presence, and gently move on to productive thoughts. Forcing away unpleasant thoughts or emotions does not work; it only makes things worse. I have used this acceptance approach with troubling emotions and thoughts, and with attendant behaviors, many times (hundreds at least) before I started to see them float away prior to causing me difficulty. Be tolerant of yourself when mistakes occur. But don't give up, as all such practice is invaluable in the inner peace work generally, and specifically with our helpers.

I mentioned above that there were two standpoints from which others can help us, one direct, which I have just addressed, and one indirect. The indirect aspect of how others can help us does not involve asking them to assist us, and can thus be very helpful for the person who does not have a helper at the moment. But the indirect method is also valuable for the person with a helper, as it adds more input for self-reflection and progress toward inner peace.

We start by becoming more astute and careful observers of our behavior and others' reactions to us. The idea is relatively simple but, as is usual with things dealing with inner development, rather difficult to do. This process requires us to examine how people respond to us in every type of situation, challenging or delightful. If we watch carefully, without judgment or defensiveness, others' reactions will provide invaluable information to us about ourselves. Such non-judgmental observations are difficult because we are used to examining others' behavior and admiring or criticizing it, but not our own. This is not about others' behaviors, but about how and why they are reacting to us as they are. This is about us discovering ourselves through others without defending or protecting our sensitivities. The goal is to see and understand.

What can we expect to see? What people say, the words, is clearly important, but more important is the huge impact of non-verbal communication that I addressed earlier in the chapter. Our best avenue for understanding what is happening with them, and through that what we might be sending, is mostly in the non-verbal cues. All of us are capable of observing what others are sending, but it requires practice to see and hear well without reaction. It is very easy to get caught up in someone's response to us that we see as wrong or inappropriate, or even offensive. This is where practice in not allowing negative emotions to impact us plays a very big role. The better we get at not being judgmental, the better able we are to observe and to draw useful conclusions for ourselves. There is no substitute for this type of practice, whether we have a helper or not.

Think about the last time you had an encounter with an angry person, a depressed person, or an exhilarated person. Can you recall all the non-verbal signals that person sent to you? We all experience non-verbal signals, but usually at an unconscious level. We have very little practice at making those experiences conscious. After a long period of paying no attention, I now regularly practice careful observation of peoples' behavior with me. Recently I have taken this effort beyond others' reactions to me, and have begun examining how they respond to each other. No judgment is involved in these observations. I am refining my ability to see what people really mean because that helps me become more effective in my own dealings with others.

The path to inner peace is paved with the assistance of others, people who care for us or those with whom we "work" indirectly. Following the suggestions I have made in this chapter can help anyone become more aware of problem behavior and how to deal with it, and thereby make progress toward inner peace. The effort is long and entails considerable difficulty and often self-inflicted suffering. Part of this is due to our attachments and stories, and part is connected to the difficulties involved in communication about sensitive issues. But the outcome is worth every bit of the effort, both for us and for those around us.

CHAPTER 6

The Power of Paradox

For many of us and for me specifically, the word paradox does not evoke comforting images. Most of my life has been spent avoiding paradoxes, which I experienced as illogical and emotionally disturbing, although I would have denied that. Yet another false story. I saw paradoxes as representing contradiction, a situation in which two (or more) ideas or positions could not possibly exist together. Among what I saw as contradictions, the worst for me was the idea that something can be both true and not-true (I am not implying false) at the same time. Any contradictions upset my view of a world both logical and scientifically valid. I rejected whole levels of existence along with the people who saw what I could not. This is what I call the simple paradox view.

Simple paradox generally sees the world in terms of contradictions that are generally not resolvable. It sees the world as made up of strictly defined unconnected categories and resists the idea of opposites co-existing, or of something being both true and not true at the same time. It provides us with an (often THE) answer, as in something is either this or that. It is opposed to the possibility of a number of conflicting answers, all of which may be valid.

Simple paradox represents a simplistic view of the world, and is thus easy to adopt and use. It sees the world in two-valued terms, usually one good and the other bad, and is often expressed with very high certainty. It fails to take into account the complexities, subtleties, and nuances of people, events, views, values, opinions and positions that characterize the real world, and thus significantly distorts reality. Simple paradox is ideally suited to separating the world into things we like and things we don't like, the stuff of suffering.

Simple paradox is most appealing when we are under stress, particularly when we encounter someone who disagrees with us. Such occasions often evoke a defensive reaction and the problems connected to that reaction. As we have seen in Chapter 2, the Threat Response automatically pushes us to narrow our focus of attention, thereby reducing the flow of information coming in to us, and closing us to others' ideas. The Threat Response also pushes us to increase control efforts, which challenges the interaction since most of us do not want to feel controlled. The sense of threat dictates that we get the outcome we "must have." This is attachment working overtime.

With my long-held simple paradox view of the world suffering arose because I was trying to shoe-horn my concept of no contradictions into a world having lots of them. My limited view, severely curtailed by what I "knew" to be true, was at odds with the way the world actually works. I resisted what reality is because I did not like it. I was attached. However, as many wise people have said, resistance is futile, and very costly.

I recall an interaction I had many years ago with a Christian when I was in college. I was an atheist at the time. Three of my false stories surfaced in the interaction: my answers are always right, Christians are crazy, and people who disagreed with me are stupid. I had to (as in big attachment) disabuse my fellow student of his belief in God. The full force of my three stories descended on him, along with considerable sarcasm and anger. He took it without replying for about 5 minutes and then bowed his head and slowly walked away. I felt totally vindicated and justified. I still carry some of the shame of that behavior to this day.

I saw no connection between him and me. There was no room for his views in my world, and if I had my way there would be no room for his views anywhere. In retrospect I realize that much of my attachment and anger was the result of fear, fear that if his view was correct, mine had to be wrong. My view had to prevail no matter what the cost, the essence of simple paradox. I exported my lack of inner peace with a vengeance. This interaction is a classic and very unfortunate example of simple paradox in operation. There were two views of the world—his and mine, and his was dead wrong. I was operating in full Threat Response mode, and nothing was going to get in my way, not fairness, not morality, not appropriateness, not reasonableness, and not kindness. And I was totally oblivious to the harm I was causing.

The second type of paradox is subtle paradox. It embraces the co-existence of opposites, and sees inner peace as in part dependent on our incorporating such co-existence into our everyday actions. Subtle paradox does not see the world as limited to linguistic categories like "good" and "bad," which can act as separators, but is open instead to the connections of all things to each other. It accepts, even relishes, that there can be many answers in a situation, even answers that appear to contradict each other. Subtle paradox embraces nuance, and appreciates gradations and small degrees of similarity or difference which allow us to see and describe the world with far more accuracy and clarity than simple paradox does. Considerable ambiguity and uncertainty exist in subtle paradox. By practitioners of subtle paradox, this is considered a very good thing. By those in need of certainty, this is considered a very bad thing.

Fully taking into account the aspects of subtle paradox when thinking or acting requires much of us. We have to be highly disciplined emotionally and mentally, eminently flexible, non-judgmental, and wide open to newness, even to awkwardness. Subtle paradox offers no answers, certainly no clear-cut and unambiguous ones. And like most aspects of moving toward inner peace, subtle paradox asks that we be more open than ever in our lives. We must have what Pema Chodron, calls "spacious mind."

Spacious mind is not just about openness, it is about curiosity as well. It is about the never-ending quest to understand ourselves, to rid ourselves of attachments and false stories, to develop inner peace. This open and exploratory attitude is exemplified in a lovely poem by musician and poet Leonard Cohen:

> Ring the bells that still can ring
> Forget your perfect offering
> There is a crack, a crack in everything
> That's how the light gets in.

Spacious mind asks that we see there are imperfections ("cracks") in everything, especially ourselves, and that such imperfections are a way to get out of the darkness and into the light of inner peace. It is the imperfections that point the way. In Western society, having a goal of perfection is often seen as commendable. That imperfection is part of the path to inner peace can be quite disturbing, and this view is a good example of the limitations of simple paradox. Other than denial, it has no way to deal with the subtle paradox that arises when we suggest that imperfection leads to something considerably better. Or, that perfection and imperfection are two sides of the same coin, that we may move back and forth between them. Is this perfect? Yes. It is imperfect? Yes.

In Chapter 3 I presented the idea that in learning we go from order to disorder and, we hope, on to further order and disorder in a near endless progression that produces greater effectiveness. Order and disorder are intimately and inextricably connected, expressing subtle paradox. We simply cannot learn well unless both operate. This is the same idea as that expressed by perfection and imperfection—we cannot have one without the other.

Simple paradox relies on the construction of distinct, mutually exclusive categories, which challenges our move toward inner peace. But not all categorizations are problematic. It all depends on how we use them. Language benefits us in allowing us to assign what we experience to categories, boxes that connect with other similar boxes, or boxes which are clearly very different. This allows us to categorize and thereby see identities, similarities and differences, and we cannot function well without being able to make such distinctions. Any animal must be able to distinguish between edible and non-edible berries, or between potable and non-potable water. We are no different.

But language's categories can be problematic for the seeker of inner peace because of the concept of two-valued reasoning. Its basis is that ideas, views, opinions, philosophies, politics, nearly everything in fact, can be put into one of two boxes, one is good and one bad. The boxes are viewed as polar opposites with nothing connecting them, simple paradox. This view sees most situations as resolvable into good or bad, right or wrong, true or untrue, like or dislike. This categorizing limits the type and amount of information we let in, when our search for inner peace demands as much openness as possible.

A friend is captured by the allure of the positive/negative categorization. It appears connected to a particular story he has told himself about his own views generally and his political party specifically. His political views are very different from mine, and he often blasts my party, although he is very nice to me while doing it. One evening I asked him if my party stood for anything good or had ever done anything beneficial. He appeared dumbfounded and simply looked at me, not at all unkindly, and remained silent. He was honestly unable to answer. Sadly, having framed his political world so narrowly and so rigidly, in simple paradox terms, he is unable to conduct a thoughtful and uplifting conversation.

This rigid filtering blocks us from a broad and deep understanding of things because our world is limited to information with which we agree. We cannot examine without fear concepts or positions that appear in opposition. My political friend does not have to believe as I do, but subtle paradox would allow him and me to converse about complex and potentially contentious issues with the only goal being greater knowledge for each of us. With subtle paradox we seek not to win, but to understand in greater depth, to understand together even while we continue to have different views. As I have said before, whether two people have different views on something is not the problem. That is the way of the world. The problem arises when the differences are carried out without respect. Relying on subtle paradox opens enormous avenues for thought and conversation. Relying on simple paradox does the opposite.

The two-valued reasoning of simple paradox shields us from hearing and fairly examining what others have to say, and often engenders resistance as well. We are wedded to our right/wrong view and thus every conversation in which we differ with another is a contest to see who "wins." Worse, this same "reasoning" curtails and often inhibits completely our ability to examine aspects of ourselves which are in the way of moving toward inner peace. Attachments and stories must see the fierce light of day for us to move forward. Adopting subtle paradox helps the light to shine, while simple paradox diminishes it.

Subtle paradox embodies the idea, prevalent in Eastern thought, that the existence of one thing automatically and instantaneously brings its opposite into existence. If I dream up the word "wet," the word "dry" immediately arises. If I say "warm," then "cold" comes into existence. These are two very obvious examples of words and their opposites co-existing, and our world is full of similar opposites. But what is less obvious is that "wet" and "dry" are not separate simply because we have named them and put them into different categories. In fact, the two words and the conditions they describe are tightly and irrevocably connected to each other. This type of thinking disturbs many of us. It seems that our world, founded substantially on linguistic names and categories (neat little boxes) and with considerable certainty thrown in, is not quite as stable as we thought.

What is this connection between apparent opposites? When we think clearly about words that appear opposite, we know intuitively that in the real world there are degrees of wetness or dryness. Picture a spectrum with absolute dry on one end and absolute wet on the other.

Absolute Dry————————————————————Absolute Wet

As we move from absolute dry toward absolute wet, or the reverse, deciding whether something is wet or dry is arbitrary. For most of us, holding such a view is not very troubling in our day-to-day lives. I can come home after getting a sprinkle on me and say with total understanding that I am wet. No great loss that I have not determined that I am wet to some degree.

But let's consider a more complex issue: the apparent polar differences between atheists and theists (of any religion). Using the image of a spectrum again, imagine moving away from absolute atheism toward absolute theism. When have we moved far enough away from atheism to become an agnostic? When have we moved further yet to become a modest theist? Or, when has a theist moved far enough to become an agnostic? None of these is determinable. The decisions are arbitrary and thus contain an inherent uncertainty. Simple paradox formulations demand that a person be one or the other, that there be no ambiguity.

Certainly any two people can occupy their respective absolutes: one a confirmed theist and the other a confirmed atheist. They might plausibly argue that they could not be more different in view from each other, and at one level they would be correct. At a deeper level each exists only because the other exists. The theist brings the atheist into existence, and vice versa. Further, there is another interesting connection between these two individuals: they are united by belief. Each believes, often very passionately, they he/she is 100% correct and in complete possession of the truth. They each share totally in belief, in absolute certainty, in simple paradox. But those beliefs do not require that they stay in simple paradox, only their attachment does this, and they can move beyond that and still maintain their separate beliefs.

It is not just words that evoke their opposites. Ideas and actions can do the same. I once consulted with a group of managers who wanted to increase workers' control over their output so as to enhance both creativity and productivity. At the same time the managers wanted to maintain an "appropriate" level of hierarchical control. In a meeting with the managers I found them to be divided into those seeking greater worker autonomy (and lower hierarchical control) and those seeking less worker autonomy (and greater hierarchical control). The two sides quickly degenerated into us-versus-them argument with resistance on both sides. Only when we established that the two concepts existed together in a necessary tension, subtle paradox, could the group begin to cohere and make progress.

Couples often end up in merry-go-round situations in which action produces resistance which produces its own resistance, endlessly. Imagine I have a deep-rooted fear of being controlled arising from childhood challenges. This deep fear is how I see much of the world, meaning I often experience others trying to control me, especially my wife, even though there may be no such intent. I am hyper-sensitive and act out a reality which is an illusion, yet another false story. Of course, I powerfully resist any perceived control, which then evokes resistance from my wife (not to mention others), which I then resist, and on and on.

Let's say that I don't want to continue the dance of resistance breeds counter-resistance, and I want to get over my control issue. But accomplishing these means that both my wife and I have to look at the problem from the standpoint of subtle paradox. The question that arises in this context is who has responsibility for my control problem. In one sense the problem is clearly mine. It arises from within me and damages others. Therapy can aid me in seeing that the problem is mine and not someone else's, and I make progress when I see that I am responsible for the inappropriate behavior and for making positive changes. But as beneficial as this understanding is, by myself I may not be able to get beyond my control issue.

In another sense, one embodying subtle paradox, my problem is also my wife's. But how can she be responsible for something so clearly my issue? She does not cause my reactions. I choose my reactions whether I think so or not. But if our desire is to aid each other in making progress in the relationship and possibly toward inner peace, I cannot move forward very easily without her help. She can make things easier for me or harder for me. Making things easier does not mean allowing me to misbehave. It means she understands the control issue that drives my behavior and actively assists me by ensuring she does not inadvertently encourage me to undesirable responses. Such quality actions on her part assume that I have been up-front with her about the challenge and have shown her that I want to change, even if for a while I still have breakdowns. My wife can continue the "push-back" style of interaction, which will help no one, least of all her. She is not responsible for my problem or its outward manifestations. But she voluntarily assumes responsibility for helping me help myself, just as I accept a similar responsibility for helping her with her issues. Subtle paradox means we are both responsible for my problem, but in different ways.

I recall at the start of the first Iraq war some people using simple paradox. One side said we are going to Iraq only to take their oil. The other side said we are going to Iraq only to provide democracy. Both of these formulations are unfortunately simple. For people of opposite views on the war these formulations preclude any elevating conversation, any meaningful dialogue. These formulations are designed for one thing: I win, you lose. And it's so much easier to make a person lose when I have reduced something to child-like simplicity. Both simple paradox formulations fail to see the subtleties and nuances that were really involved, no matter whether a person supported the war or not. Folks with such simplistic views have been captured by the tyrant of certainty, resulting in a near total elimination of the ability to have quality conversations about the war. Folks prone to this type of "thinking" in one area, say the war, are very likely to apply it in other situations, resulting in more suffering.

This example illustrates a critical aspect in our search for inner peace. Both those opposed to the war and those in support constructed simple paradox formulations, and that compromised their ability to see through to the complexities and nuances of the issue. Closer to home, we are asking others (our helpers) to assist us in our search for inner peace. Framing the world in either/or terms, in simple paradox terms, is very dangerous. At the very least a simple paradox view will seriously constrain the conversation, and at worst it could destroy the relationship with our helper.

Additionally, interacting with others in general when we frame the world in this way can engender interpersonal problems, since not everyone will agree with our views. My regrettable experience with the Christian illustrates this dramatically. Often when we frame the world in simple paradox terms we do considerable harm to others. This framing also challenges the idea and spirit that part of our movement to inner peace is to act in ways with others that are uplifting both for them and for us, to export our inner peace. Challenging conversations, where there is considerable disagreement and often plentiful emotion, must be managed by us for the wellbeing of all. As I discuss in Chapter 7, simple paradox views undermine our ability to ensure both quality conversations and the wellbeing of others because it evokes resistance and pits one view against another in a "fight-to-the-death" experience.

Regrettably, simple paradox formulations seem to allow us to "win." We reduce a very complex issue or person to a singularity (either good or bad), claiming essentially that this formulation represents the whole of the person or the issue. Looking at things in a more sophisticated manner, with subtle paradox, requires us to deal with considerable uncertainty and ambiguity. For many of us, especially those with a high need for certainty, simple paradox formulations are our bread and butter. They allow us to feel certain, and at one level to avoid the sensations attending uncertainty and ambiguity. But at a more sophisticated level, suffering is very much part of this way of living.

Typical (or not) paradox statements:

- Something is beautiful or ugly.
- You are a good person or a bad person.
- People work hard or they don't.
- You love me or you don't.

- You can't have anything unless you let go of everything.
- The more you know the less you understand (Tao Te Ching).
- The more things change the more they remain the same.
- Less is more.

The first four examples are clearly different from the last four. The former has the word "or" in them, conveying simple paradox: you can have one but not the other. It is easy to see the "either/or" formulation even though "either" is not expressed, and herein lies the problem with simple paradox. Either/or formulations serve to reduce the complexities of issues, people, events, etc., to only two aspects, neither of which can tolerate the other. Each of the two aspects of simple paradox is incomplete, and may be incorrect as well. Most of us know that the world is not really built that way; people, issues, and events are usually far more complex and subtle than can be conveyed in a two-valued, simple paradox expression. We certainly think of ourselves as being quite complex. But under stress (often arising when we are confronted with those whom we do not like or whose views we do not like) we often revert to a simple either/or formula that does nothing to explain anything in depth, and usually distorts the issue. To make matters worse, we are often strongly and emotionally aligned with one side of the simple paradox and equally strongly opposed to the other side. Our view is correct and any opposing one is incorrect.

The set of four subtle paradoxes that follows the simple ones is much more interesting and of great value in our search for inner peace. Thinking about the four examples can be taxing as they seem to express things that make no sense at all, at least in the Western view of paradox as contradiction.

Yet each one expresses a profound truth about the way reality operates. The more we can appreciate and live in these truths, and those of other subtle paradoxes, the more progress we will make on the path to inner peace. We must be able to see reality as it is, which is expressed by subtle paradox, accompanied by the glories of uncertainty and ambiguity.

To bring the value of paradox home, let's look at paradoxes many of us experience with our spouses or life partners.

Privacy and transparency.
Personal control and shared control.
Freedom and restraint.
Individuality and community.

Seen from simple paradox, these are "either/or" propositions. Imagine your spouse or life partner telling you that you don't get any privacy as he/she sees that everything has to be transparent. Not very appealing at all. But seen from subtle paradox, they are "both/and," giving any relationship much more complexity and potential value. In any loving relationship, there is a necessary constant tension between these pairs in which both operate simultaneously and benefit the parties. Forcing one or the other to prevail ensures a challenged relationship and suffering.

I have mostly portrayed simple paradox in a bad light, but it is often helpful, even necessary. There are many times during any one day, perhaps for nearly all of it, when we are going about our normal activities and there is no need for an attitude of subtle paradox. I don't mean that we should forget the value of subtle paradox, but that it does not have to occupy our every conscious moment. Normal interactions with others can be of a very simple, and perfectly healthy, nature. The "wet"/"dry" example I gave above is a case. We do not need to concern ourselves endlessly over whether we are partially wet, a lot wet, or soaked. Saying to another that we are wet is fine. In the give and take of everyday existence this is perfectly normal and does not have to constrain our movement to inner peace.

But developing further on the path to inner peace does require attention to and an attitude of subtle paradox in at least 2 situations. The first is how we frame and talk to ourselves about the world. We want to monitor our thoughts and emotions as we allow in more and more information about ourselves that is often difficult to accept. We want to ensure that simple paradox does not cause us to see things in defined and opposing categories, which will restrict our openness and our movement to inner peace.

Another situation asking for the attitude of subtle paradox relates to challenging situations and challenging people. These can push us into becoming judgmental (simple paradox) or attached to a particular outcome. Early on the path we are at our weakest when hit with such challenges. It is then that we must see reality as it is, and restrain ourselves as best we can from unpleasant thoughts, emotions or actions. Simple paradox is very enticing when we feel threatened, angry, or insulted, but only subtle paradox will help us to retain our inner peace and act as a force for good. Staying balanced and in the present moment is so challenging when we encounter conflict that I devote all of Chapter 7 to dealing with difficult situations.

So, what is the power of paradox? An attitude and practice of subtle paradox allows us to frame the world and our presence in it in the most expansive way, and to open ourselves to valuable information about ourselves, our views, and our relations with others. Subtle paradox encourages us to see the world not from the standpoint of categorizations, but from the standpoint of connections. It thus becomes a very big factor in both the development of inner peace and becoming a force for good.

The practice of seeing multiple sides to issues, including apparent contradictions, aids us in removing the tendency most of us have to assign a good/bad value to things, to categorize. As we invest less energy in categorizing and more in seeing the subtleties and complexities inherent in nearly everything, we find it easier to connect with those with whom we disagree. Gradually we see that the world in its fullness can be grasped only with subtle paradox.

CHAPTER 7

Conversations That Really Work

For most of my life I had very few ways of looking at interactions with others. Mostly I viewed them as contests in which I was right and the others were not, and in which I had to prevail. As we have seen in earlier chapters, this behavior expressed my lack of inner peace and kept me from being a force for good. My great need to win meant that my information gathering was very limited. In situations with no disagreements I more or less paid attention to the content, but in a desultory way. In the case of contests, which I managed to find nearly everywhere, my information gathering was finding weaknesses in the other's positions or arguments. I was most concerned about whether I was winning or not. In neither type of conversation was I particularly concerned about the wellbeing of the other person. And in a contesting conversation I had a vested interest in the diminished wellbeing of my "opponent." If I thought I was losing, very unpleasant emotions arose, causing me to misbehave even more.

We have all been in difficult conversations, ones that are filled with negativity. For some folks most of their interactions with others are like this. Regrettably, resolving differences constructively and respectfully, even between people who love each other, is not much in evidence today. Conflict interactions are stressful and may easily push us into undesirable behaviors. They are like battles, with a winner and a loser. And like any zero-sum game, what you gain comes at my expense and vice versa. And even the "winner" cannot relax, because the game never ends and he/she may lose next time around. Suffering for all.

Developing inner peace is hindered when we engage others in battles, and it is very difficult under such circumstances for us to be a force for good. Certainly we can avoid challenging interactions, and occasionally that is warranted. For most interactions, however, we can and should be present and helpful. This chapter is about engaging others in respectful and compassionate ways, especially when disagreement or hostility is present. It is about how to develop a conversation that flows easily and in which both parties are elevated, are uplifted.

As I said in Chapter 1, inner peace is about inner clarity, which is the purity of our connection to reality unencumbered by our false stories, likes and dislikes, and attachments. The purer our connection to reality, the greater our inner peace. Assisting others in finding greater clarity, without attempting to change or control them, is part of how we show compassion and respect for them. We can offer clarity as a gift in a conversation without any expectation that it will be accepted (and often it will not be), an important contribution we can make to being a force for good.

Gaining inner peace and becoming a force for good are the two vitally important aspects of a healthy existence. Gaining inner peace may require that we have valuable conversations with a helper, which I addressed in Chapter 5. While this chapter is about more general conversations, ones we encounter every day, the suggestions for creating positive outcomes can definitely be used in helper conversations. These conversations can be used both for practice in maintaining balance (gaining greater inner peace) and for being a force for good, for exporting inner peace. I am using "conversation" to apply generally to any interaction we have with one or more people, whether it is problematic or not.

Conversations take different forms, from the silly to the causal to the practical to the deeply philosophical or academic. They cover every topic under the sun, and we have many each day. We are unlikely to have our inner peace or our goal of being a force for good tested with each one. But every day we are likely to have a few occasions in which one or both of these is tested, and it is important to know how to deal with those in the most productive and respectful way.

Interactions in which disagreement or hostility is present can most easily push us off balance and out of inner peace. With the right mental and emotional attitude, however, and with compassion for the other in our mind, we can maintain inner peace and be a force for good no matter how difficult the conversation. I have emphasized a number of times that conflict is only a difference in view which need not be unpleasant, and can be very enjoyable. But when people are attached to their views, harm to others nearly always occurs because their view is challenged and may evoke a Threat Response, leading to a diminished and rigid conversation. We are looking to develop conversations that are respectful and open, uplifting and supportive.

I mentioned in Ch 2 that differences of opinion or view can become negative when we have one or more of the following goals:

- To inform the other that he/she is wrong or incorrect without having a very good reason.
- To persuade the other to change to our way of thinking or acting.
- To punish the other for having a view different from our own.

The third is unfortunate for obvious reasons. The first two are problematic because they usually arise from a position of certainty, leaving no room for open and exploratory conversation, or for resolving a difference in perspective in a way that benefits both. The underlying dynamic with informing and persuading is often control and winning, with suffering often arising. Informing and persuading can be beneficial, but far less often than most people think.

I have a simple rule regarding when I need to actively and directly intervene to inform, contradict or rebut in a disagreement situation. I will do so only if what is happening (or likely to happen) is patently illegal, clearly immoral, or if someone will be hurt. I have found that in excess of 99% of my challenging interactions do not meet any of these requirements. This includes conversations in which people want me to weigh in on an important and weighty issue about which they may have strong positions. In such circumstances I try to engage others in ways intended to reduce tension and enhance well being, all the while helping move the conversation to ever more respectful and expansive levels.

The most important requirement for us in problematic conversations is to keep our balance, for us to be firmly in the present moment. Even conversations that have no serious challenges for us still ask that we remain balanced, as that is an integral part of our daily life of inner peace. If we are not in the present moment we are unlikely to act well in a conflict interaction. And this gets at the second requirement, that of being a force for good by exporting our inner peace in conversations.

Since being a force for good means we engage others in the most productive and respectful ways, we must manage our behavior so that any conversation flows more expansively and uplifts all participants. It does not necessarily mean we agree with what is being said. When I have conversations now in which my views are different from the other person's, outcomes are generally good. I do not hold my views or positions with a level of emotion (attachment) demanding that I attack or defend. My views do not have to prevail. In fact, often I do not even present my views. Since there is no need for me to parade my views or force them on others, there is little that can present conflict.

Our ability to successfully be a force for good in a challenging conversation depends on a number of factors, one which I have already mentioned—staying balanced and in the present moment. We can manage a conversation for the good of all if we are aware of our own inner dynamics, what we feel and what we think, and ensure those do not adversely affect the interaction.

A second factor is our ability to see and hear everything that is going on in the conversation, the content, the words, and the non-verbal cues. We have to know what to look for and how to use that information wisely and compassionately to move the conversation forward. What does the other person appear to need? What do the non-verbal signals tell us about the person's state of mind and intention? Is he/she angry, excited, certain, amused, etc? What do these signals mean for moving any challenging conversation forward? As I have pointed out, the greater our ability to gather information from others, the more options we have for working successfully with them. Those options result from our being clearer both about what is happening and how we can deal with that most respectfully.

When we maintain our balance and treat others with respect (even while they may not be treating us with the same respect), we inject an important type of clarity into a challenging interaction, what I call emotional clarity. This clarity arises from our calm inner state, undisturbed by negative emotions. Emotional clarity often brings down the level of emotion or irrationality in the interaction and is accomplished both by what we say and how we say it (all the non-verbal elements, most particularly voice tone). If our voice is calm and soothing, our body language soft and supportive, and our words careful and not attacking, we inject emotional clarity into the conversation.

Clarity is also added in the more usual sense of the word when we engage others in content discussion or analysis, what I call content clarity. We learn little when we make statements, and we learn the most when we ask questions. Questions serve to elevate our knowledge and to assist us in exporting our inner peace. Using questions allows the other participants, even when very upset (sometimes with us), to explain a particular point without having to worry about being attacked. With that safety, we can often see them visibly relax, an important non-verbal clue. There can be a beautiful flow to such conversations, even under trying conditions. Questions may also help the others understand the conversational differences in a new way without necessarily having to change their opinion.

Most people cannot maintain their anger or hostile disagreement in the face of no defense and non-attack, especially when we offer the opposite of attack: care and gentleness. A key in such settings is to avoid giving others something with which they will upset themselves, which will contribute to their lack of inner balance and clarity. Expressing negative emotions, making provocative statements, or asserting that the other is wrong will ensure trouble, a diminishing of both emotional and content clarity. Even people who are in a combative frame cannot do much when there is nothing for them to swing at. It is like trying to hit air.

To illustrate my points about good and not-so-good conversations, and how to help with interactions that could (did) go badly wrong, consider the following dialogues.

A couple my wife and I know had put their house up for sale, and experienced a bit of interpersonal difficulty:

A: Have you spoken to Judy (realtor) recently?
B: Yes. I spoke with her yesterday about the possibility of reducing the price a little.
A: Hey, aren't I part of this decision as well!
B: Of course, why in heaven's name would you think you are not?
A: We never agreed we were going to reduce the price and I resent that you did not discuss this with me before you spoke with Judy.
B: Oh, come off it! I never told her to reduce the damn price. I only asked if she thought we should.
A: What do you mean, "Oh, come off it"! Don't even think about patronizing me!

This is a not uncommon marital difference in which neither party behaved particularly well, with the conversation quickly degenerating. In this dialogue, A (he) gets agitated very quickly before understanding what B (she) had or had not done. She then quickly gets exasperated, saying unhelpful things and expressing a dismissive tone of voice which further upsets him. This brings him into a totally different realm of content: his perception that she was condescending to him, which she may well have been.

What might have worked better?

A: Hey, aren't I part of this decision as well!

B: Sure. I didn't mean to sound like I had made a decision on my own to reduce the price, and I am sorry if it came across like that.

A: You mean there was no agreement between you and Judy to reduce the price?

B: That's right. I was interested in getting her view so that you and I could discuss it.

A: Thanks. I'm sorry I got a little agitated.

It's clear that both parties controlled themselves in the second series. She handled his potential disruption carefully and very respectfully. The key is that she does not become hooked by what may be an over-reaction by him, who then realizes all is OK after asking a clarifying question, and then apologizes for his agitation. Ideally in this situation he would not have reacted initially as he did. He would have asked the clarifying question right away (did a decision get made without him?). Still, each tried to connect with the other's concern and soothe any ruffled feathers as well, both dealing with a legitimate issue and helping the relationship.

A fellow I know lives in Portland, OR and he has an old friend who lives in Seattle. The latter would come and visit three or four times a year, mainly when on a business trip. The visitor stays with his Portland friend during these trips. Here is a phone conversation about the Seattle friend's upcoming Portland trip:

A: I am looking forward to your visit. I always enjoy having you stay.

B: I can't stay this time as I have to be closer to the convention center. Also, I have to spread my material all over the place, and I don't want to mess up your place.

A: You're kidding, of course! You won't mess anything up and you always stay here.

B: I do always stay with you and really enjoy it, but can't do it this time.

A: Well, I hope you know this really hurts my feelings.

What happened? A placed his own needs over the well being of his friend. The friend's needs were irrelevant. He wanted the friend to stay and any thwarting of that represented an insult and a minimization of the friendship. That the friend cannot make an occasional exception to staying demonstrates a real problem in the Portland man's view of the relationship, and a not very healthy one at that. A person with more balance, understanding and inner peace may have responded as follows:

A: I understand. I wish you could stay, but I know there will another chance on your next trip.
B: Thanks so much for understanding. I really do look forward to our get-togethers.

Two friends go to a movie and after have the following exchange:

A; What did you think of the movie?
B: I thought it was awful.
A: Why?
B: The protagonist was not real, the music did not fit with the story, and the dialogue was very poor.
A: Was there anything good about it or anything that interested you?
B: Nothing.

We all have conversations like this from time to time, and they seem quite normal. And they are, unfortunately, all too normal. This is not an uplifting conversation. It is barely a conversation at all because the responder blocked the conversational movement at every point. But we might argue that the responder has every right to not like the film, and that is true. The problem here is not the dislike of the film. It is the failure to use the film as a springboard to good conversation and an enhancement of the relationship. How could the responder been more uplifting and elevating?

A: Was there anything good about it or anything that interested you?
B: I can't really think of anything. What did you think?
A: I liked the plot, particularly when the protagonist was faced with having to choose between two actions, neither of which was appealing.

The responder (B) has a choice to make here, whether to stay insistent in his view or to move the conversation to a higher level. We know what will happen if he stays certain in his view and that is all he expresses. But let's say he decides not to block, but to expand the conversation.

B: I had not thought of that side. Having two options, neither of which is very attractive, does present an interesting moral issue. How do you think the protagonist could respond with those kinds of constraints?

This conversation is now moving right along, uplifting both parties and expanding the inquiry into the film. Notice the value of questions in moving things along productively.

Above I mentioned that the huge majority of any disagreements are of no significance at all. Consider the following set of dialogues:

A: That house has been for sale for 6 months.
B: No, it's been for sale for 5 months.
A: I recall our great trip to Italy in 2005.
B: No, we went in 2006.
A: I think we have a new mailperson.
B: Nope, still the same one.

What do all of these have in common? First, whether one view is correct or not is of no consequence whatsoever. Second, the responder in each case has negated the first speaker's observation. Third, the negation is not necessary. Nothing is gained by the denials, the flow of even a very short conversation is abruptly halted, and any chance of having an uplifting exchange is diminished or destroyed. Consider changes that could be made to enhance the interaction and improve the relationship quality:

A: That house has been for sale for 6 months.
B: It's sure been a while, hasn't it? I hope they get it sold.
A: I recall our great trip to Italy in 2005 with great fondness.
B: Was it really 2005? Or 2006? Whatever year it was, we had a grand time.
A: I think we have a new mailperson.
B: Really, I didn't know that. Have you seen the new person?

The revisions show a much more pleasant interaction. Suppose the person responding in the second series still holds the views actually expressed in the first series. Meaningless. She understands that those views are unimportant, and acts appropriately. The positive result of this caring response is more respect and a small but important enhancement of the relationship. The responder in the second series is in control of her behavior, sees what will work in the conversation, and attends both to the various issues and to the well being of her partner. Further, her considered remarks open the way to more conversation on each of the issues. Consider where just one of the dialogues might go:

A: I recall our great trip to Italy in 2005 with great fondness.
B: Was it 2005? Or 2006? Whatever year it was, we had a grand time.
A: What was your favorite place?
B: Florence, without a doubt. How about you?
A: Santa Margherita.
B: Do you think you'd like to go back?
A: Sort of, but I might prefer Spain this time.
B: I'm not sure on Spain, but I'd love to hear why you'd like to go there.

Obviously this is not a momentous interaction, but it flows elegantly and smoothly. It builds the relationship because both parties are careful and supportive of each other, each assisting the conversation in becoming more expansive and uplifting. A true sharing of inner peace and clarity.

Hold on a moment, you might say. What about issues that have some or a great deal of importance to the participants? A very good question, and the answer is the same as for inconsequential issues: very seldom does it matter enough to have to directly counteract the other. As I have said before, disagreement is not a problem unless it is carried out disrespectfully. Can we disagree without being disagreeable? Certainly. Let's look at an important conversation going awry and how it could go better.

A: I am really upset that the governor's budget cuts more money from the higher education budget.
B: What are you talking about! Colleges and universities waste all kinds of money.
A: Get real! You can't run these educational systems like a business. Our young people's futures are at stake.
B: And so I suppose you expect that we pay no attention to value and cost.
A: Of course I think those are important, but the state budget for higher education has been cut now for nearly 4 years in a row. This is no time to be worried about possible, and I say possible, waste.
B: So what that the budget has been cut for the last 4 years! Those same colleges got tons of state and Federal money for decades all the while raising tuition like there was no tomorrow.

This conversation is about a very important issue: funding for higher education. But it's going nowhere fast. Each has a powerfully-held view that cannot be altered (certainty!), and the other's view has to be challenged and preferably destroyed. There is no inquiry, no expansiveness, and little evidence of respect—a very messy situation, lacking any type of clarity. But improvement is possible with a little care.

A: I am really upset that the governor's budget cuts more money from the higher education budget.

B: Higher education has taken some big hits recently, but what can we do during a serious financial crisis?

A: I agree that it is a financially troubling time, but aren't we damaging our young people's future to deal with a short-term financial issue?

B: There is something in what you say, although I have a deeper concern. Higher education has been receiving a lot of money from both states and the Federal government for decades. During that time they have been raising tuition at a 7% per year rate. Isn't it possible that we can use this time of lower budgets to adjust for the possible excesses?

A: I do understand we cannot sustain that level of increase. My concern is addressing the disappearance of majors, the increase in class sizes, and the increases in student loans that will be needed as it takes students longer to get their degrees.

B: I see your point about our young people's futures being possibly compromised. Fewer classes could mean longer time needed to graduate and possibly increased debt as well. Do you think we could look at how to help with these things and at the same time address waste?

This conversation is healthy, respectful and expansive. The positions did not become solidified. Each felt no need to defend, and this led to a much more positive interaction. Each affirmed the other. And it may also lead to new views about funding for higher education. There is no reason any conversation cannot go this well, and there are some important things we should do (or refrain from doing) to aid that effort.

First, as I have said, the most important thing is to be in the present moment, fully attentive to the other person. Second, it is best not to present our views from a position of certainty or in a provocative manner (do not give others something to swing at). Being careful in this way means we avoid generating opinion battle lines which then have to be defended at all costs. This idea is conveyed nicely by Michael Kahn in his fine book, *The Tao of Communication*: "I want to suggest that there is very little payoff in embattled conversations. People learn very little, they change their positions hardly at all, and they come out of such conversations feeling something between uncomfortable and terrible."

Third, it is important to affirm the other party. We do not have to agree, but it is important to acknowledge the other and any good points made, particularly if those conflict with ours. In the above conversation B did a good job of affirmation after A mentioned the upset with the cuts. It is lovely to be in a conversation and hear the person who disagrees with us say something like, "That is a really good point. I had not thought of the issue in those terms." Building on what the other has said is also very helpful: "As you said . . . ,'or "A minute ago you raised a really important point." None of these comments requires that we change our views, that we agree with the other person, only that we use respectful techniques to aid the conversation and those in it.

Fourth, use questions carefully to elevate and move the conversation in a positive direction. Questions give us a chance to assess what is happening in the conversation as well as add to our knowledge. Fifth, adopt an attitude that the conversation is to get greater clarity about a complex issue and to enhance the relationship, no matter how short that is. With clarity as the guiding factor, there is no need for anyone to win or be right. Even if others in the conversation seek the latter, we do not have to. We can manage our own behavior such that both we and they are uplifted. We must choose in every interaction: are we seeking to win or do we want an uplifting and expansive conversation? We cannot have both.

For example, if I say, "I think welfare is a mess," I am just asking for someone who disagrees to go on the offensive and contradict me. Battle lines are immediately drawn and the attack/defend process begins. I am being provocative and very likely seeking an "I-win, you-lose" interaction, or at least to unsettle my "opponents." But what if I think exactly that about welfare? The key is not to hide what I think but to present it carefully, perhaps indirectly, and perhaps not at all. Why not present my views? Better to ask, "Why do I need to present my views now, or at all" if the goal is an uplifted conversation? Could I address welfare without being provocative? What if I simply asked a question: "Do you think there are any aspects of welfare that could be improved?" This very general question helps me get the conversation going before defenses come up and allows me to determine where the other person stands, both emotionally and in terms of how she thinks about welfare.

Imagine she says in response to my question, "Not really. There may be a few inefficiencies, but I think it pretty much works well to help those in need." She does not feel threatened at this point, and this allows me the next question: "Do you think there is a point at which people on welfare can be damaged by becoming dependent on it?" Notice I don't frame this as people will be damaged, only that they might be, and that after some time. And it is phrased as a question, not a statement or assertion.

She could respond, "There may be a few, but I think most people would prefer to get off of welfare. What do you think?" She has asked my opinion, which is an indirect affirmation and a bit of encouragement, and I need to decide how best to proceed. Telling her she is wrong, or that I disagree in some way, will produce few expansive benefits, so I respond, "I agree that most people are unlikely to want to stay on welfare for a long while. What do you think we should do about those, and we don't know how many they are, who could be damaged by a long-term reliance on welfare?" I was able to honestly validate her position and then move into a question of what shall we do with the few that are in danger (there may be many, but that is irrelevant as the issue is how to assist anyone from becoming dependent on welfare).

But what if I have data about welfare that may contradict her view. So what? If I use that data my goal has changed from having an uplifting and learning interaction to something else, such as to inform her she is wrong, to change her view, or to punish her, all of which often derive from a less-than-respectful place. Likely she will respond with her own data, and now we have what I will loosely call a "crap-throwing contest," with the last person standing being the "winner." Suffering and no help on the path to inner peace.

One last example from a quite challenging interaction. I met a fellow at a party not long ago who had very pronounced views of folks with my political party affiliation. Below is a short piece of our conversation. This is an example of a situation that could be very hostile if I fail to keep my balance.

A: I cannot believe how stupid (_____'s) are!!!
B: Really. What makes you think so?
A: All their positions on everything from abortion to unions to gay marriage. They're idiots.

B: There does seem to be a lot of disagreement in today's society, wouldn't you say?

A: Absolutely, and it's the fault of those damn (_____'s).

B: I have noticed that divisiveness as well, in just about any arena. Did you see any of that in your line of work (he was a teacher in K-12)?

A: Oh, lots. In the classroom you have economic, racial, life-style, all kinds of differences.

B: Did those translate into divisiveness?

A: Sadly, they did. I had trouble negotiating the mine-field of difference and so did the students.

This conversation, which started out in a way that could be combative, is now flowing along. I had to make a decision early on whether to stay with the conversation at all. I gave it a bit of time and saw quickly that talking about (_____'s) was not going to be fruitful. So, I very carefully used questions to alter the focus of the conversation by moving it to something he knew about and had experienced. We were now talking about divisiveness in schools, and not about (_____'s). This is what I mean when I talk about "managing" a conversation for the good of all. The suggestions I made in Chapter 5 for working with our helper bear repeating because they are valuable in any conversational setting:

- Ask questions that help clarify what the other is saying.
- Make few if any statements.
- Avoid defending oneself (As in, "Let me tell you why you are wrong").
- Refrain from outright disagreement, even if the other is incorrect.
- Address only the issue being presented and no other.

Every conversation, casual or complex, easy or hostile, is a chance for us to practice being in the present moment, for us to acquire inner peace. Each conversation is also a chance for us to improve the quality of any relationship we have with another person, to be a force for good, even if the interaction is only seconds or minutes long. Most important is the work we do with our helper, and the conversations illustrated in this chapter can be additional models for that work.

Being balanced and disciplined we have the ability to "manage" the conversation to the benefit of all and without any need to change or control them, mainly by injecting emotional and content clarity into the conversation, and by being careful in how we bring up and respond to issues or challenges. Not all negative interactions will work out easily or as well as I have portrayed some in this chapter, but our manifestation of inner peace will show in the care and respect we show for the other person, the most important thing we can do as a force for good.

CHAPTER 8

Compassion and Wisdom, Pillars of the Uplifted Life

We achieve inner peace by giving up our attachments, false stories and likes and dislikes, giving us a profound sense of calmness and detachment. We accept the world as it really is, not wanting it to be other than it is. And we become a force for good by exporting that inner peace to others. However, being such a force is only possible if we develop compassion and wisdom, the two great pillars of an uplifted life resulting from our work on inner peace. The first part of this chapter will be about compassion.

As we have seen, compassion is often seen as sympathy or empathy for another's plight, which is certainly a valid perspective. But in the Eastern world the term is more expansive. As I mentioned in the Introduction, my favorite definition of compassion is from the Dalai Lama: "Compassion can be roughly defined in terms of a state of mind that is nonviolent, nonharming, and nonaggressive. It is a mental attitude based on the wish for others to be free of their suffering and is associated with a sense of commitment, responsibility, and respect towards the other."

Embodied in this definition are three very important elements. First is the idea that our basic state of mind (includes the unconscious) should be empty of any aspects of harm. As we have seen with inner peace in general, this state of mind is not arrived at easily. Many people at the conscious level see themselves as not harmful, but their unconscious may have other agendas. Second is the sense that we wish others to be free of their suffering, just as we wish to be free of ours. Third is the idea that we accept a responsibility to other human beings to assist them in moving away from their suffering.

The commitment to compassionate action is easier said than done. To act out our care for others requires that we have attained some level of inner peace. Lacking that, it is nearly impossible to aid others, for we will have failed to aid ourselves and will thus look hypocritical. Worse, without inner peace our actions could easily become intrusive and controlling, generating resistance. Our intentions will be good but the outcomes will not be.

For many years I envisioned myself as, if not really compassionate, at least sensitive to others. Sadly for myself and others, I was not. I have given examples earlier of my lack of compassion, and here is another. I started full-time work after the military with the US government. A group of us were friends and we saw each other socially. One of my colleagues brought in a large coffee-table-sized book of impressionist art. I still shiver when I think of my comment: "Oh, in two months you'll be able to get that for half the price." I thought I was being funny, although no one else thought so. I certainly had no intention to harm her; I was simply oblivious to her well being and to my human connection to her. My need to appear funny and to be noticed trumped her well being.

Compassion does not arise simply because we have decided we want to have it. Only in conjunction with the efforts we make to find inner peace can we develop compassion. The connection of inner peace to compassion is relatively straightforward. Moving to inner peace asks that we accept reality as it is, without our attachments and likes and dislikes. It means we examine ourselves and our behavior and become aware of our lack of inner clarity and its outward expression. It asks that we use discipline and practice to alter our inner selves and how we act toward others, a transformation that will be visible to others and which will positively affect them, even if only indirectly. Compassion arises as we practice inner peace because we embrace others without reservation, understanding that their well being is of the utmost importance.

After the unfortunate incident I related above, I did little to change my orientation to others, even while I was reading wonderful Eastern thoughts on compassion. I realized I was not acting very compassionately around the same time I recognized that I did not have much inner peace and was exporting that lack to others. My efforts to achieve a higher level of compassion met a lot of resistance as I had grown up as an only child and for the most part had only one way of seeing things: what was for my benefit.

It is very common to have our world upset by interactions with others who present problems. As we practice acceptance of others we are disciplining our minds and emotions in a way that provides the foundation for compassion. But compassion is not only about a state of mind, it is also about action. What does acting compassionately look like in general?

We are acting compassionately toward others when we:

- Are wholly present for them.
- Non-judgmentally and respectfully accept them.
- Offer them our trust and care.
- Create safety for them (particularly when they suffer).
- Express humility.

Every interaction does not call for all of these actions. When I pay for my parking ticket at the airport the only thing I want to do is create a short, uplifting connection by smiling and offering a thank you, even if the ticket-taker is not in a good mood and offers nothing positive to me. I am expressing care for that person, and that is fine for that interaction. When we are having an easy conversation with an old friend often little more is needed than our caring attention.

But other interactions require more. As a force for good expressing compassion we approach and interact others with respect and openness, even those who are angry, fearful, jealous, envious, whose state of mind and emotions are negative and causing them to suffer. Such people bring tension and conflict to their interactions, and our goal is to aid them in removing their suffering, always without expectation that the change will happen and without the need to control them. As I mentioned in the last chapter, our compassionate actions depend on our being able to "manage" conversations in a way that uplifts them and the interaction.

Since all interactions will be different, compassion asks that we see things from a variety of viewpoints. Especially in conflict situations we must put ourselves in the mind of the other person. This is not about agreeing with what the person is doing or saying, only about understanding without judging, about seeing as best we are able from that person's viewpoint. This understanding leads us to successfully choose the most helpful and uplifting options for dealing with a particular situation.

Some may think that other people's lack of inner peace is none of our business and trying to change that an impossible task even if it were our business. It may well be an impossible task, still our commitment to the well being of others calls us to action, but this action is unique. It has no goal. The action is an offering, a gift to others with no expectation of acceptance or of appreciation. We are not attached to changing anyone, to them behaving or thinking differently. There is no effort to control them. We are acting out our inner peace and our commitment to be a source of assistance to all people. They may accept or reject the offering, and both are alright.

There is an interesting connection between humility and compassion. In the West we often think of humility as self-abasement or having low self-esteem. Excessive humility can indicate these things, but real humility is a far cry from them. First, humility comes from understanding the nature of reality, that all is transient, including us. This allows us to see that there are very few really important things, and our ego definitely isn't one of them. Second, it arises when we firmly hold the value that all human beings are worthy of respect and care, and that we are no better or worse than anyone else. Third, humility exists when we embrace the idea that we share with all humans a desire to be happy (have inner peace) and to alleviate our suffering.

If we adhere to these elements we act from real humility because our actions arise from the sense that we are all in this together and we all strive for the same important things. This keeps us from pushing ourselves to the front, from taking credit, from demanding that others see our views as right, from demeaning those who do not act or think as we do, from seeing ourselves as better or more important than others. Having humility does not mean we cannot have a realistic (as opposed to an exaggerated) sense of our competence and abilities. Nor does it mean we are patsies and have to take whatever others dish out. But we must keep in mind that no one can insult us, anger us, make us look foolish, or embarrass us unless we let them. If we do let them, we are expressing our own inner turmoil and lack of inner peace and clarity. More suffering.

Compassion and humility are blocked when we take ourselves too seriously, when we assign our views, opinions, or actions an importance they do not deserve. Considerable emotion is invested in this importance and we are then in a "must have" situation that practically assures suffering. We live in fear that others will not take us seriously, and we thus manufacture a false story of who and what we are. We are now in a state where we want what we want and opposition is not tolerable. We have placed so much emotional value (seriousness) in being something that we are not that we are thrown off balance at the mere thought of not being taken seriously. In taking ourselves and our desires too seriously we cannot act compassionately because we are consumed with getting what we want. The wellbeing of others is not something we think about, and it is actually a problem because it takes our attention and emotion away from focusing on what we want.

Having humility does not mean we have no ambition or on occasion, competitiveness. Neither of these is inappropriate. Ambition and competition are about striving, and there is nothing wrong with this unless we are attached to the striving or to its outcomes. Can we strive mightily and possess inner peace and humility? Absolutely. It is not the effort that is the issue, it is the attachment which will cause us to do harm.

The martial art of aikido (variously defined as The Way of Harmony of the Spirit) has lessons for dealing compassionately and humbly with those who may wish us harm. A critical part of aikido is blending, in which you bring your opponent very close to you and then take actions allowing you to escape the attack while not harming the opponent. The non-harm ethic is vital to aikido, and in that moment of closeness to your attacker you see the situation from his point of view. In his fine book, *The Way of Aikido*, George Leonard also talks about verbal blending, in which, " . . . instead of meeting a verbal attack with a verbal counterattack you respond first by coming around to your attacker's point of view . . . ." Leonard makes clear that blending physically or verbally allows us to see many more options for handling a challenging interaction. He even goes so far as to say, "It could be said that the health of an individual or an organization is generally proportionate to the number of perceived options at its command." This idea is similar to the one I advanced earlier in the book about having maximum options to deal with difficulty and that such options are only developed by a wide-open and fearless gathering of information.

Our ability to "manage" interactions allows us to engage without hostility and at the same time to protect the other person. My example at the end of the prior chapter about a man I had met at a party who disliked folks with a particular political view is a good illustration of "management" that keeps harm from happening and also protects and uplifts the other participant. In that case his energy was primed for battle and he began the interaction with a frontal attack. But I presented him with no opposing force, no counterattack. Instead, through careful and gentle "management" I assisted him in redirecting his energy toward a more positive and uplifting purpose. Acting compassionately in difficult situations is hard, but can be achieved with the same discipline and practice that we apply to our growth to inner peace, and this leads us to wisdom.

Wisdom is one of those concepts that most of us think we understand, at least we sense we know it when we see it. But we often hold very different views of what wisdom is, how it is demonstrated, and how it is acquired. There are hundreds of definitions, many of which offer a glimpse of what wisdom is. We can also try to explain wisdom using a list of character traits, aphorisms, anecdotes, or quotes, which often provide considerable insight into aspects of wisdom. We can point to famous individuals we believe possessed (or possess) wisdom, such as The Buddha, Jesus, Socrates, Marcus Aurelius, Abraham Lincoln, ML King, Nelson Mandela, and Mahatma Ghandi. But there is no one definition, aphorism, or person defining wisdom conclusively, and that includes all the wise quotes I have used in this book.

There may be some disagreement with my last statement because "ultimate wisdom" exists in Buddhist thought, referring specifically to our acceptance of the transient nature of things. We might call this the "great" definition, and getting closer to inner peace requires that we have this acceptance, at least to some degree. Still, if we are to act beneficially, there is more to wisdom than the acceptance of transience. At the practical level, where we can be a force for good on a daily basis, we have to look at wisdom a bit differently. In this more mundane (but not at all unimportant) sense wisdom is inner peace and compassion in action.

More specifically, my offering to the long list of definitions is: Wisdom is how we overtly express inner peace and compassion to others, and how we aid them in reducing suffering.

While many views of wisdom have benefits, there are three views that can be an obstruction to a true appreciation of wisdom. The first is that wisdom is the accumulation of knowledge, as when a person knows a great deal about something, such as fixing a car, programming computers, raising children, designing homes, serving the homeless, or even meditating. Wisdom of this kind, knowing a lot about a particular thing or process, is extremely valuable and makes the world go round. I recall an older friend of my parents who could prune trees beautifully. I would watch and he would tell me what he was doing and why, such as not letting two branches cross each other and how to determine which one to snip. This type of knowledge is wonderful and eases our transition through life. When people possess knowledge they freely pass on in a way that benefits others, that certainly can be considered the expression of wisdom at some level.

But my sense of wisdom is that it is broader, deeper, and has as its primary goal the well being of others at all times and in all circumstances, not just when knowledge is being passed. This type of wisdom is not dependent on accumulated knowledge in a particular area of life, but on inner peace and compassion accompanied by what I call wisdom-specific knowledge (addressed below) which is translated into action for the good of others.

Earlier in the book I referred to a wonderful quote by Shunryu Suzuki which relates to our knowledge discussion. He says, "In the beginner's mind there are many possibilities, but in the expert's there are few." As we use the term, an expert is someone who knows a lot about something, explaining why people may see a knowledgeable person (an expert) as a wise person. But being an expert is not without dangers. We may think our knowledge defines the world, and become arrogant and rigid in our thinking, the opposite of what we need to do to move toward inner peace.

When knowledge is seen as THE answer (certainty again) moving to inner peace is seriously obstructed. I have mentioned a challenge many of us have in the search for inner peace—confusing the inputs to inner peace with the presence of inner peace itself, something I did for decades. I have friends who have a deep knowledge of Eastern traditions, which they can quote and discuss with ease and erudition. They truly know what they are talking about; they are very knowledgeable. But they have not connected the wisdom of those teachings of how to live and relate well to others to their own lives, yet they imagine they have achieved inner peace and wisdom. The wonderful things they know have not penetrated to their personal lives. They know that they know, but they do not know that they do not really understand, and thus are living a false story that impedes their progress to inner peace and wisdom.

This book emphasizes the radical need for awareness and an ever-greater appreciation for what we don't know, especially about ourselves. We cannot act as a force for good while fooling ourselves about ourselves, holding onto false stories and maintaining attachments. We must nourish and support the beginner's mind, the one that is open, endlessly curious, flexible, and fearless, one that is directed to wisdom. Knowledge by itself, no matter how profound, will not produce inner peace or wisdom.

A second view that compromises a real understanding of wisdom is related to the first one. If wisdom is the accumulation of knowledge, it fails to see that the latter can be used for both good and bad, whereas wisdom as I define it can only be used for good. A horrific use of knowledge can be seen in the Nazi death camps, put together by people very knowledgeable of how to efficiently and ruthlessly kill thousands of people very quickly.

Lastly, there are people who believe that expressing compassion will suffice for all difficulties we face with others, and thus in their minds compassion constitutes wisdom. Being compassionate, having a non-violent mind, as the Dalai Lama says, is a profoundly important aspect of our development toward inner peace, but by itself will not always allow us to effectively deal with challenges arising from troubled interactions we have with others. We also have to know what to do and how to do it while acting for the benefit of all, something I have endeavored to provide in this book. With relatively simple challenges, the mere expression of compassion will do quite well. But for more challenging ones, we need additional resources.

And this leads to the requirement for wisdom-specific knowledge, entailing four elements. To be a true force for good, to act with wisdom, we must have knowledge of:

- Ourselves at a deep level.
- The fact and forms of our and others' suffering.
- How to move beyond suffering.
- The methods for being a force for good no matter what the situation.

Increasing our levels of understanding of these will enhance our sense of inner peace and compassion. Most importantly, such understanding enables us to act for the wellbeing of others, what I consider the prime expression of wisdom.

I suggested in Chapter 1 that inner clarity describes the purity of our connection with reality, and it has a profound relationship to wisdom, which is the outward expression of our clarity. As we practice getting to inner peace and greater compassion, and acquire the wisdom-specific knowledge needed to implement those, clarity automatically arises. We are clear when our thoughts, emotions and actions are aligned with what is, when the proper action arises spontaneously. Nothing extra is added, only that which is needed and no more, all with the wellbeing of others in mind. This clarity demonstrates economy of thought, emotion, and action. Physical and emotional energy is wasted when we try to keep the real world at bay, when we try to maintain our illusions. With wisdom we waste no energy trying to maintain false stories or attachments, nor trying to figure out what to do or say in a particular situation. It is all there, and presents itself with no effort and literally no thought.

Being able to respond so adeptly and helpfully is my personal goal, and what I want to inspire in readers. I have made some progress in this wisdom effort, but I have a ways yet to go. In the past I would blurt out whatever would come to mind at the moment, helping or hindering others was of little consequence. Now, I think much more carefully about what to say and how to say it, whether the situation is challenging or not. I desire to progress to a point of development where what to say and how to say it arise automatically, and my response is exactly right for the well being of all—a place where no thought is needed.

As I have suggested throughout the book, the path to inner peace is a very difficult one, demanding perhaps the greatest effort of our lives. But the biggest hurdle may not be the work, but the transition from one who does not see to one who is willing to see, and to act on that. All movement forward depends on our fearlessly accepting at the beginning of our journey that we have blind spots which are causing us and others problems. This acceptance must be on faith because we cannot see them yet, and our attitude toward these blind spots must be that others can see them (at least to some degree) and can thereby be of help to us. Any rejection of the idea that these blind spots exist and exert significant negative force on us, and on our relations with others, means progress to inner peace will be severely, if not terminally, obstructed.

At the start of the book I provided some characteristics of people who have achieved inner peace, setting the stage for what we all wish for ourselves. Throughout the book I have made the point that the precondition for doing the right thing at all times is the presence of inner peace and compassion. The various chapters have defined the hurdles to inner peace and the possible ways around those hurdles, including very practical applications and practices. I explained why compassion arises automatically as we practice the path to inner peace. We can now see that as important as developing inner peace and compassion is, it is only when those are implemented in our daily lives that we can truly say we are acting from wisdom.

The basis of all movement to inner peace, and ultimately to compassion and wisdom, is openness. Lacking it, we simply cannot progress, no matter how strongly we wish to alter our inner and outer selves. The poet David Whyte expresses this beautifully in his poem, Opening of Eyes:

> It is the opening of eyes long closed.
> It is the vision of far off things seen for the silence they hold.
> It is the heart after years of secret conversing speaking out loud
> in the clear air.

Can we open our eyes long closed?

USEFUL RESOURCES
AND REFERENCES

I received inspiration from all of the following fine books. Those I mentioned directly in the text have an asterisk.

The Art of Happiness, HH The Dalai Lama and Howard C. Cutler, M.D.*
Beyond Rational Management, Robert E. Quinn
Buddhism Without Beliefs, Stephen Batchelor
Comfortable With Uncertainty, Pema Chodron*
Contemplative Science, B. Alan Wallace
The Five Things We Cannot Change, David Richo
The Essence of Alan Watts, Alan Watts
Everyday Suchness, Gyomay M. Kubose
Everyday Zen, Charlotte Joko Beck
Happiness, Mathieu Ricard*
The Happiness Hypothesis, Jonathan Haidt
Happy for No Reason, Marci Shimoff
Images of Organization, Gareth Morgan
The Joy of Living, Yongey Mingyur Rinpoche
The Light Inside the Dark, John Tarrant
Mindsight, Daniel J. Siegel, M.D.
No Self, No Problem, Anam Thubten
On Being Certain, Robert A. Burton, M.D.
Passages, Gail Sheehy*
The Places that Scare You, Pema Chodron
Primal Leadership, Daniel Goleman*
Simple Taoism, C. Alexander Simpkins and Annellen Simpkins
The Stoic Art of Living, Tom Morris
Strangers to Ourselves, Timothy D. Wilson

Taking the Leap, Pema Chodron
The Tao of Conversation, Michael Kahn, Ph.D.*
The Unencumbered Spirit, Hung Ying-ming
The Way of Aikido, George Leonard*
The Wisdom of Insecurity, Alan Watts
Wisdom of the Peaceful Warrior, Dan Millman*
Yojokun, Kaibara Ekiken
Zen Mind, Beginner's Mind, Shunryu Suzuki*

www.ingramcontent.com/pod-product-compliance
Lightning Source LLC
Chambersburg PA
CBHW030359290526
45785CB00004B/1821